Bede Griffiths
an autobiography

THE GOLDEN STRING

With my prayers

Bede Griffiths

9:9:92

Templegate Publishers

Published by:
Templegate Publishers
302 East Adams Street, P.O. Box 5152
Springfield, Illinois 62705

ISBN: 0-87243-126-6

To Richard
to whom this book owes its existence

FOREWORD

It is now twenty-five years since *The Golden String* was written
and nearly fifty years since the experiences which I have
recorded took place. During this time a great many changes
have taken place in my own life, in the Church and in the
world. In my own life the most important event has been
my coming to India, which has changed my outlook both on
the monastic life and on the Church and on the world.
When I wrote *The Golden String* the boundaries both of the
Church and of the monastic life and their relation to the
world seemed to be fairly fixed, but since the Second
Vatican Council the whole perspective has changed. The
Roman Church has opened itself to the other Christian
Churches, to other religions and to the secular world in a
way which has created a new situation and established a
new relationship. In a sense these changes had been
prepared in my case by the Biblical, the Liturgical and the
Ecumenical movements, which had shaped my thought
when I was writing *The Golden String*. But Vatican Two has
carried these movements further than I would ever have
expected. Biblical criticism, Catholic and Protestant alike,
has advanced to a point where we have to see the whole
Biblical revelation in a new light. The Liturgical movement,
by the introduction of the vernacular instead of the traditional Latin, has opened the Roman Church to other
cultural traditions in a way which must gradually change
the very structure of the Church. The Ecumenical movement, by opening to other religions, has brought the Church
into contact with other religious traditions in a way which is
producing a radical change in the relation of Christanity to
other religions.

The most radical change which has taken place has been
in the understanding of the temporal and historical character of the Bible and the Church. The Bible, instead of being

regarded as a fixed and final revelation of God to man, is seen as a historic process in which the Word of God is being revealed under changing historical conditions, shaped by the historical, psychological and cultural circumstances of a particular people, and Jesus himself has to be seen as the Word of God "made flesh" under the conditions of a particular historical situation. In the same way the dogmas of the Christian faith can no longer be regarded as fixed and final statements of Christian faith, but as expressions of Christian faith, guided by the Holy Spirit, but always conditioned by particular historical circumstances and capable of ever new expression. Christian theology has developed so far under the influence of Greek and Roman thought and in terms of European culture. It is only now that we are beginning to see the possibility of a Christian faith interpreted in the light of Asian and African experience, leading to a new understanding of the Church in the light of other religious traditions. It is obvious that the place of the Roman Church, which has been the guardian of the Greco-Roman tradition and a centre of unity for those who follow that tradition, will be modified. The old system of Roman Catholicism with its uniform liturgy, theology and canon law has already passed away and a new understanding of the Church as a communion of churches, united in faith and charity but with a diversity of liturgies and theologies, is now accepted.

A Catholic may see the growth of the Papacy, like that of Episcopacy, as the work of the Holy Spirit in the Church, but he will see it as something conditioned throughout by historical circumstances. The structure of the Papacy inherited from the Middle Ages is already passing away, and we may expect to see a development of the Church which will take it nearer to the Church of the fifth century, when there were Syrian, Egyptian and Greek churches representing Asia, Africa and Eastern Europe, each with their own liturgy, theology and canon law, united with the Latin Church of the West and recognizing a certain primacy in the Church of Rome as the See of Peter. If this conception is extended today to embrace the different cultures of Asia and Africa as well as those of Europe and America, one can conceive of a Catholic Church which would be really "catholic", that is, universal, uniting the different churches of East and West with their diverse cultural forms and structures in one body, and engaged in dialogue with other religious traditions. What would be the basis of unity in such a church? Could it not be the simple formula of St Paul: "One Lord, one faith, one baptism and one God and Father of all"? The later forms of doctrine and discipline in the different churches were "developments" of Christian faith, and there is little hope of uniting the different churches on the basis of such developments. The essence of Christian faith is expressed in the simple formula of the early Church – "Jesus is the Lord", of which St Paul wrote that "no one can say that Jesus is the Lord except by the Holy Spirit". It is, then, the faith in God as Father, in Jesus as the Lord, in the Holy Spirit as the witness to the Lordship of Christ, which would be the common faith of all Christians, and the sacrament of Baptism in the name of the Father, the Son and the Holy Spirit which would be the visible sign of their unity. The sharing in a common Eucharist would be the sign of the love which unites the disciples of Christ in their common faith and hope.

But this still leaves open the question of the relation of the Church to other religions. I would not now speak as I did of an "absolute" religion or an "absolute" Way. There is only one absolute religion and that is the religion of the Holy Spirit, which is the Spirit of Love, present in some measure in every religion and in every man, and drawing all men into that unity for which man was created. There is only one absolute Way, which is the Word of God, that Word which is God himself, communicating himself to man and making himself known "in many and various ways" to different peoples. That Word was "made flesh" in Jesus of Nazareth, but he does not cease to make himself known to other people in other ways. So also the Holy Spirit, which descended on the disciples at Pentecost and continues to dwell in the

Church, does not cease to work in other people and to dwell among them in other ways. All religions are historically conditioned and though the absolute may be found making itself known and communicating itself in a religion, the religion itself can never be "absolute" in the sense of being free from historical and cultural conditions. We have to recognize the presence of the Word of God and the Spirit of God in all religions and indeed outside all religions, while we acknowledge the unique revelation of the Word made flesh in Jesus Christ and the unique manner of the dwelling of the Holy Spirit in the Church.

If there is a new understanding of the Bible and the Church today, there is also a new understanding of the secular world. The Church today sees itself not so much as set in opposition to the secular world as at the service of the world. But even more important than this is the change which is taking place in the understanding of the secular world itself. When I and my friends sought refuge from the Industrial Revolution and made an experiment in simple living in a Cotswold village, we were simply responding to our own personal need to find a more meaningful way of life. But since that time the whole world has begun to discover the disastrous effects of the present system of industrialism. The exhaustion of the earth's resources, the pollution of earth and air and water, the monstrous growth of nuclear power, are all threatening to destroy the planet and it is becoming clear to all who can see that our present civilization is set on a course which is leading to disaster. The conditions of life in a modern city, which set man in conflict with nature, also set him in conflict with himself. The result is a psychological tension, which must lead either to a destructive war or to an internal breakdown or to both. In other words, we are beginning to experience on a world scale the same kind of situation as led to the breakdown of the Roman Empire. But at the same time a new hope has dawned. A revolt against the whole system has begun among the new generation and a recognition that a new beginning must be made. This movement extends through-

Foreword

out the world among people of all religions and of no religion. It is a movement towards a science and a technology which will cease to exploit nature and will learn to live in harmony with nature. It is a movement also towards a more human way of life, in which human relations are seen to be of more importance than material progress and efficiency, and the quality of life more important than large-scale organization for material ends. Finally, it is a movement towards a unified vision of life, in which man and nature are seen to be part of a cosmic order – what in ancient India was called *rita* and in ancient China *Tao* – an order of life which relates man both to nature and to the eternal realm of transcendence, on which man and nature both depend.

When I wrote the Prologue to *The Golden String*, I had begun to compromise with Western science and industrialism, and to imagine that they could be used "in the service of God". But I now think that this is an illusion. The present state of the world is not due to some defect in the use of science and technology, which can be corrected. Western science and technology are based on a false philosophy which has undermined the whole of Western civilization. It is based on the belief, of which Descartes was the spokesman in the seventeenth century, that there is a material world, extended in space and time, independent of human consciousness, and that the human mind can examine this world objectively and so arrive at a knowledge of "reality" which will give him control over the world. This view has now been proved false by science itself, but the old-fashioned view of science and reality still dominates the ordinary man in the West. Marxism is only an extreme form of this illusory view of reality and the whole of the Western world is more or less subject to it. There can be little hope therefore that Western science and technology will change their basic character. The only hope lies in a deliberate break with the whole system and an attempt to reconstruct science and technology on a new basis. This will only come when the Western world has undergone a radical change of consciousness – a change which will probably be accompanied by a breakdown of the present system – and has recovered the wisdom of the ancient world, the world not only of Christian Europe but of India and China and Islam. Unfortunately India and China and the Arab world are now exposed to the full force of Western science and technology with all its devastating effects. The new world must therefore be the creation of East and West together seeking to recover the wisdom which has been lost and to advance into the new age now beginning.

THE GOLDEN STRING

I give you the end of a golden string;
Only wind it into a ball,
It will lead you in at heaven's gate,
Built in Jerusalem's wall.

WILLIAM BLAKE

One day during my last term, at school I walked out alone
in the evening and heard the birds singing in that full
chorus of song, which can only be heard at that time of the
year at dawn or at sunset. I remember now the shock of
surprise with which the sound broke on my ears. It seemed
to me that I had never heard the birds singing before and I
wondered whether they sang like this all the year round and
I had never noticed it. As I walked on I came upon some
hawthorn trees in full bloom and again I thought that I
had never seen such a sight or experienced such sweetness
before. If I had been brought suddenly among the trees of
the Garden of Paradise and heard a choir of angels singing
I could not have been more surprised. I came then to
where the sun was setting over the playing fields. A lark
rose suddenly from the ground beside the tree where I was
standing and poured out its song above my head, and then
sank still singing to rest. Everything then grew still as the
sunset faded and the veil of dusk began to cover the earth.
I remember now the feeling of awe which came over me. I
felt inclined to kneel on the ground, as though I had been
standing in the presence of an angel; and I hardly dared to
look on the face of the sky, because it seemed as though it
was but a veil before the face of God.

These are the words with which I tried many years later

to express what I had experienced that evening, but no words can do more than suggest what it meant to me. It came to me quite suddenly, as it were out of the blue, and now that I look back on it, it seems to me that it was one of the decisive events of my life. Up to that time I had lived the life of a normal schoolboy, quite content with the world as I found it. Now I was suddenly made aware of another world of beauty and mystery such as I had never imagined to exist, except in poetry. It was as though I had begun to see and smell and hear for the first time. The world appeared to me as Wordsworth describes it with " the glory and the freshness of a dream ". The sight of a wild rose growing on a hedge, the scent of lime tree blossoms caught suddenly as I rode down a hill on a bicycle, came to me like visitations from another world. But it was not only that my senses were awakened. I experienced an overwhelming emotion in the presence of nature, especially at evening. It began to wear a kind of sacramental character for me. I approached it with a sense of almost religious awe, and in the hush which comes before sunset, I felt again the presence of an unfathomable mystery. The song of the birds, the shapes of the trees, the colours of the sunset, were so many signs of this presence, which seemed to be drawing me to itself.

As time went on this kind of worship of nature began to take the place of any other religion. I would get up before dawn to hear the birds singing and stay out late at night to watch the stars appear, and my days were spent, whenever I was free, in long walks in the country. No religious service could compare with the effect which nature had upon me, and I had no religious faith which could influence me so deeply. I had begun to read the romantic poets, Wordsworth, Shelley and Keats, and I found in them the record of an experience like my own. They became my teachers and my guides, and I gradually gave up my adherence to any form of Christianity. The religion in which I had been brought up seemed to be empty and meaningless in comparison with that which I had found, and all my reading led me to believe that Christianity was a thing of the past.

An experience of this kind is probably not at all uncommon, especially in early youth. Something breaks suddenly into our lives and upsets their normal pattern, and we have to begin to adjust ourselves to a new kind of existence. This experience may come, as it came to me, through nature and poetry, or through art or music; or it may come through the adventure of flying or mountaineering, or of war; or it may come simply through falling in love, or through some apparent accident, an illness, the death of a friend, a sudden loss of fortune. Anything which breaks through the routine of daily life may be the bearer of this message to the soul. But however it may be, it is as though a veil has been lifted and we see for the first time behind the façade which the world has built round us. Suddenly we know that we belong to another world, that there is another dimension to existence. It is impossible to put what we have seen into words; it is something beyond all words which has been revealed.

There can be few people to whom such an experience does not come at some time, but it is easy to let it pass, and to lose its significance. The old habits of thought reassert themselves; our world returns to its normal appearance and the vision which we have seen fades away. But these are the moments when we really come face to face with reality; in the language of theology they are moments of grace. We see our life for a moment in its true perspective in relation to eternity. We are freed from the flux of time and see something of the eternal order which underlies it. We are no longer isolated individuals in conflict with our surroundings; we are parts of a whole, elements in a universal harmony.

This, as I understand it, is the "golden string" of Blake's poem. It is the grace which is given to every soul, hidden under the circumstances of our daily life, and easily lost if we choose not to attend to it. To follow up the vision which we have seen, to keep it in mind when we are thrown back again on the world, to live in its light and to shape our lives by its law, is to wind the string into a ball, and to find our way out of the labyrinth of life.

But this is no easy matter. It involves a readjustment to reality which is often a long and painful process. The first effect of such an experience is often to lead to the abandonment of all religion. Wordsworth himself was to spend many years in the struggle to bring his mystical experience into relation with orthodox Christianity and it may be doubted whether he was ever quite successful. But the experience is a challenge at the same time to work out one's religion for oneself. For most people today this has become almost a necessity. For many people the very idea of God has ceased to have any meaning. It is like the survival from a half-forgotten mythology. Before it can begin to have any meaning for them they have to experience his reality in their lives. They will not be converted by words or arguments, for God is not merely an idea or a concept in philosophy; he is the very ground of existence. We have to encounter him as a fact of our existence before we can really be persuaded to believe in him. To discover God is not to discover an idea but to discover oneself. It is to awake to that part of one's existence which has been hidden from sight and which one has refused to recognise. The discovery may be very painful; it is like going through a kind of death. But it is the one thing which makes life worth living.

I was led to make this discovery myself by the experience which I have recorded at school. This was the beginning for me of a long adventure which ended in a way for which nothing in my previous life had prepared me. If anyone had told me when I was at school or at Oxford that I should end my life as a monk, I should have doubted his sanity. I had no idea that any such thing as a monastery existed in the modern world, and the idea of it would have been without meaning to me. I have tried to show, however, that the steps which led to this revolution in my life, though they were in some ways exceptional, nevertheless followed a logical course, and I hope therefore that they may be found to have more than a personal interest.

I was one of those who came of age in the period after the first world war, and I shared its sense of disillusionment at the apparent failure of our civilisation. In an effort to escape from the situation in which we found ourselves I was led, with two Oxford friends, to make an attempt to " return to nature ", and to get behind the industrial revolution. The attempt was, of course, in one sense, a failure, but it led to the unexpected result that I made the discovery of Christianity. I read the Bible seriously for the first time, and found that the facts were quite different from what I had supposed and that Christianity was just as much a living power now as it had ever been. I then had to find a Church in which I could learn to practise my new-found faith, and after a long struggle, which cost me more than anything else in my life, I found my way to the Catholic Church. From that it was but a short step to the monastic life, and so by successive stages a radical change in my life was effected. In recording these stages I have tried to show how each step was accompanied by a long course of reading, in which all the reasons for the change were worked out.

In this way I was forced to reconsider all the historical steps which have led us into the present situation. We have progressed from the rejection of the Church at the Reformation, to the rejection of Christ at the French Revolution, to the rejection of God at the Russian Revolution, until we are now faced with a world which is in danger of destroying itself both morally and physically. If we are to escape destruction, we have to find our way back again to the point from which we started and to make the discovery first of God, then of Christ, and finally of the Catholic Church.

This rediscovery of religion is the great intellectual, moral and spiritual adventure of our time. It is something which calls for all our energies, and involves both labour and sacrifice. But it cannot be a mass movement. The discovery has to be made by each individual for himself. Each one approaches it from a different angle and has to work out his own particular problem. Each alike is given the golden string and has to find his own way through the labyrinth. But there are certain problems which are common to us all. We have all to take account of the new world in which we live. We cannot simply go back to the past; history is irreversible. We have to make the discovery of God in the light of our modern knowledge, of all that physics, biology and psychology have to tell us. We have to see the significance of Christ in relation to the whole of that vast sphere of time which history and anthropology now open to us.

Finally we have to see the Catholic Church, not merely as one among many Christian sects, or even as one form of religion. We have to see Catholicism, in the words of a great French Jesuit,* as "religion itself", as "the form which humanity must put on, in order finally to be itself". Somehow we have to find a form of religion which can transcend all the differences which now divide us and unite not only all Christians but all mankind in the service of Truth itself. If I have seemed sometimes to neglect these considerations and to speak as though "modern science" and "modern civilisation" were simply to be rejected, I hope that it will be understood that I am describing a phase through which I had perhaps inevitably to pass, and that the final goal which lay before me was not their rejection but their integration with religion.

Paradoxical though it may appear, it was the monastic life which made me realise this, as nothing else could have done. A monastery can never be merely an escape from the world. Its very purpose is to enable us to face the problems of the world at their deepest level, that is to say, in relation

* H. de Lubac, *Catholicism*, Burns, Oates & Washbourne.

to God and eternal life. Everything in the monastic life down to the minutest detail has to be viewed from this angle.

A monastery nowadays has to be largely self-supporting, as St Benedict originally intended it to be. This means that it is necessarily involved in those problems of economic life with which our civilisation is faced. I thought at one time that the ideal would be to do without the use of the products of industrialism altogether, but I was soon forced to realise that this was impossible and that the real problem was how to make use of science and industry in the service of God. In the same way a monastery cannot cut itself off from modern social problems. It has to find its place in the framework of a civilised society, and the challenge of such forces as Nazism, Fascism and Communism, and the more immediate challenge of our own social system, must inevitably affect it. It has, indeed, within itself potentially the seed of a new social order. As an organised form of community life, based on manual labour, and seeking to bring every form of human activity into direct relation with the service of God and of one's neighbour, it has its own definite contribution to make in the shaping of a new world.

We know that the monasteries were responsible more than any other institution for laying the foundations of the medieval world, and it is not impossible that they will have a similar role to play in the future. St Benedict lived in the last days of the Roman Empire in a world which bore a striking resemblance to our own. Civilisation was threatened alike by disintegration from within and by violence from without. It was his work to act as a bridge between the old and the new world. His rule formed the basis of a way of life which was able both to preserve the traditions of the ancient world and to lay the foundations of a new civilisation. Now that civilisation is once more threatened with destruction, may it not be that the monastic order may once again help to preserve the tradition of the past and to build up that new world which is surely being born out of all the labour and struggle and pain of the world today? However that may be, it is certainly true that monasticism offers today, no less than in the past to those who are called to it, a life in which the search for God through the integration of one's whole being is made the dominant motive of life.

That search for God which began for me on that evening at school has gone on ever since. For the more one discovers of God, the more one finds one has to learn. Every step in advance is a return to the beginning, and we shall not really know him as he is, until we have returned to our beginning, and learned to know him as both the beginning and the end of our journey. We are all, like the Prodigal Son, seeking our home, waiting to hear the Father's voice say: " This my son was dead and is alive again; was lost and is found ".

It is only now after thirty years that the full meaning of that which was revealed to me that day at school has become clear to me. That mysterious Presence which I felt in all the forms of nature has gradually disclosed itself as the infinite and eternal Being, of whose beauty all the forms of nature are but a passing reflection. Even when I was at school I had been fascinated by that passage of Plato in the Symposium, where he describes the soul's ascent on the path of love; how we should pass from the love of fair forms to the love of fair conduct, and from the love of fair conduct to the love of fair principles, until we finally come to the ultimate principle of all and learn what Beauty itself is. But I have learned what Plato could never have taught me, that the divine Beauty is not only truth but also Love, and that Love has come down from heaven and made his dwelling among men. I know now the meaning of St Augustine's words, " O thou Beauty, so ancient and so new, too late have I loved thee, too late have I loved thee ". I know now that God is present not only in the life of nature and in the mind of man, but in a still more wonderful way in the souls of those who have been formed in his image by his grace. I had sought him in the solitude of nature and in the labour of my mind, but I found him in the society of his Church and in the Spirit of Charity. And all this came to me not so much as a discovery but as a recognition. I felt that I had been wandering in a far country and had returned home; that I had been dead and was alive again; that I had been lost and was found.

CHAPTER ONE

CHRIST'S HOSPITAL

I was born on 17th December 1906 of a typical English middle-class family and was brought up in the Church of England. My grand-parents on both sides came from farming stock, but in the great industrial expansion of the nineteenth century they went into business. My mother's father rose to be an alderman of the City of London, and though I never saw him I was impressed from an early age by a portrait of him in court dress, which always hung in the dining-room. My father was taken into an uncle's business when he was still a young man, and made a partner in the firm. After his uncle's death my father himself took a partner, but this partner managed to get the business into his own hands, and in spite of a law-suit which he brought against him, my father lost all his money. I was only four years old when this happened, and I have no recollection of it. My father never recovered from the blow. He had considerable powers of mind and might once have taken a part in public affairs. But he never became reconciled to his loss and lived entirely in the past. He spent his time in endless argument on religion and politics and society, and made life difficult for my mother by his refusal to co-operate. But he had the kindest and most generous nature, and never thought or spoke ill of anyone. It was characteristic of him that he never said a word against his partner and continued to regard him as his friend to the end of his life. He had a simple, evangelical religion, and a devotion to Moody and Sankey's hymns, which he was never tired of singing. He had a pleasant tenor voice and was always a handsome man with his fair moustache and clear blue eyes. He kept the heart of a child to the end.

18

As a result of this loss of fortune we moved from Walton-on-Thames, where I was born, to the village of New Milton in Hampshire, on the borders of the New Forest and not far from the sea. Here we lived a wild, open-air life, which was for me of almost unclouded happiness in spite of our poverty. There were four of us children, of whom I was the youngest, and my mother had only a tiny income of her own; but she set to work to make a home for us, and she managed so well that, though we had few luxuries, we were never actually in need. She did practically all the work of the house herself, though she had not been brought up to it and it must have been a heavy burden, although we children were brought up to help in everything. From the age of six or seven I can remember having to make my own bed and clean my shoes and help to get the meals, to wash up and sweep and dust the rooms. I used to take a pride in it and I have always been thankful that I was made used to work and comparative poverty so early. There was an atmosphere of ordered peace and security in our lives, which seems to have passed away from life generally after the Great War. Even the war did not seriously disturb this peace for us, as we were living all the time far away in the country and neither I nor my brothers were of age for military service.

All this time my mother worked without respite, but she had her reward. Not long before her death she told me that in these early days when she had been working very hard and was beginning to feel at the end of her strength, she looked one day into the glass and saw herself surrounded by a strange light, which did not seem to come from any natural source. I have no doubt that it was so, and that it was a sign of God's blessing on her life. She rarely spoke of her religion but it was the mainstay of her life. When I think of her now it is as I used to see her often when I came into her room, kneeling by her bed, as she had done regularly night and morning throughout her life. She had grey hair as far back as I can remember, and a strong face with deep-set brown eyes, and a pronounced "Hapsburg" nose, an inheritance from the family of Henry Fielding, the novelist, to which we were related on one side.

We were all brought up to go to the village church every Sunday. The Rector was a country parson of the old school, a tall, thin man with a pointed beard, and no roof to his mouth, which made his utterance laboured but very distinct. He preached short sermons of about ten minutes in length, which was rare in those days. They were always prefaced with the words, "A few words only", and gave general satisfaction. He himself was a good man who might have stood for a portrait of Chaucer's village parson. He was a lover of nature, and used to spend days in the New Forest collecting specimens of flowers and mosses, and turned the old rectory garden into a regular bird sanctuary. He was also, as I afterwards discovered, a student of Shakespeare, whose plays he believed were written by the Earl of Oxford, and he looked with some contempt on those he called "Stratfordians". From him I learned a love and respect for the Church of England, which is interwoven with all my earliest memories. It was part of that stable background of life, which one never questioned or doubted.

Of any religious instruction I can only remember that when I was six or seven an old friend of my mother, whom we used to call Mimi and who was like a godmother to us all, made me learn the Beatitudes and the tenth and fourteenth chapters of St John's Gospel by heart. I doubt whether they meant anything to me at the time, but they have remained engraved on my memory ever since.

The services in the village church were Low church, but when I was fourteen we moved to Sandown in the Isle of Wight, and there I encountered a High church service for the first time. We used to go to a little church at a place called Yaverland, where there was a sung Eucharist every Sunday, and this made a deep impression on me; but how much it was an æsthetic attraction and how much religious, I would not like to say. For by this time I had begun to read for myself, and my reading was to draw me gradually away from the Church and eventually from any recognised form of religious belief. I began to read Scott and Dickens and Thackeray, when I was eleven or twelve, but it must have been when I was about fifteen that I began to think for myself.

My brothers and I had been sent to a preparatory school called Furzie Close at Barton-on-Sea, near New Milton, and from there we went on to Christ's Hospital, the Blue-Coat school, where Coleridge, Lamb and Leigh Hunt were educated. It was one of the grammar schools founded by Edward the Sixth to take the place of the old monastic schools, and unlike most of them it retained not only its traditional Tudor dress, consisting of a long blue coat, with leather girdle, knee breeches and yellow stockings, but also its original character as a charity school. It is unique among English public schools in that payment is made according to income and no one may enter whose parents have more than a certain amount. It was intended primarily for the "relief of the poor", so that there were boys of all classes, and no class distinctions were recognised. I have always been grateful for this, as it made it impossible for me to accept such distinctions in later life, especially at Oxford, where the sense of belonging to a privileged class was so strong.

Lamb has left a rather forbidding description of the school in the *Essays of Elia,* but all school discipline was harsh in those days. Many years later I discovered that Edmund Campion, the Jesuit martyr, and Dom Augustine Baker, the English Benedictine monk, author of *Holy Wisdom,* one of the great classics of English spirituality, were both boys there under Queen Elizabeth. But neither Catholicism nor monasticism had any place in my life at that time, and I never heard their names mentioned.

In 1902 the school was moved from its old site in the

City of London to Horsham in Sussex, not far from the modern Charterhouse of Parkminster, though I was quite unaware of its existence. The first headmaster there was a Dr Upcott, a man of the character of Arnold of Rugby, who made it into a great public school of the traditional English pattern. He impressed us all with his flowing white beard and red gown of a Doctor of Divinity, and instilled into us a real respect for the "religious, royal and ancient foundation of Christ's Hospital", as it was called from its foundation under Edward the Sixth. The religion was of a severely Protestant kind, which would, no doubt, have had the approval of its royal founder. It consisted of services each day in the week and twice on Sundays in the school chapel, which was decorated with some magnificently colourful paintings by Sir Frank Brangwyn, illustrating the Acts of the Apostles. I remember sitting for years beneath the figure of St Stephen being martyred in a gorgeous orange robe. We accepted the school chapel as part of the normal routine and we enjoyed the singing, but otherwise I don't think that it entered much into our lives. Perhaps the readings from the Bible, to which we listened day by day, affected us more than we knew, and we were all presented with a copy of the Revised Version at a solemn service on our last day at school; this certainly impressed me deeply, and I have kept my copy to the present day. Apart from Scripture classes we received no religious instruction. When I was confirmed I had to learn the Catechism of the Book of Common Prayer by heart, but neither I nor my housemaster who listened to me repeating it took any interest in it. My mind was by that time moving in quite another direction.

Dr Upcott was succeeded by W. H. Fyfe, now Sir William Fyfe. He was the first headmaster who was not a clergyman, and he introduced a new spirit into the school. In appearance he reminded me when I first saw him of President Wilson, who was then at the height of his power after the 1914 war. Mr Fyfe had been a Fellow of Merton

College at Oxford and was later to be Principal of Queen's University, Ontario, and then of the University of Aberdeen. He was a great humanist, a classical scholar, but modern in all his ideas and possessed of an ubiquitous sense of humour. His influence on us older boys was immense, and his kindness to me in particular has continued, in spite of all the changes in my life, down to the present day. He first taught me to think for myself and encouraged all my awakening interest in literature, art and politics. He was himself a socialist, like his brother, who was then the editor of the *Daily Herald,* and I shall never forget how when we were reading Plato's *Republic* with him I first began to see Socialism as the expression in modern life of Plato's ideal. In religion he was a Christian humanist, and he used to preach sermons unconventionally from the lectern in the middle of the chapel, which held us spellbound. But he did not believe in dogma, and one day in a Greek Testament class, when we challenged him on the Virgin Birth, he simply replied : "But does it really matter?" But he set before us the ideal of the humanity of Christ in such a way that it has remained with me all my life.

He was responsible among other things for enlarging the school library and opening it up to the boys, and this soon became for me the most absorbing interest of my life. I found there complete sets of Fielding and Jane Austen, of Meredith, Conrad and Hardy. There was also a facsimile edition of the first folio Shakespeare and an illustrated edition of *Paradise Lost.* These I devoured with passionate enthusiasm at every spare moment of the day. We lived in large day rooms where fifty boys were left free to read or play, but no amount of noise could disturb my reading. At night I used to take a book into the bathroom, which was the only place where a light could be kept on with impunity, and I remember reading *Paradise Lost* in this way with the book propped up against a board across the bath.

There was probably a good deal more enthusiasm than discrimination in all this reading, but it affected me profoundly none the less, and gradually shaped my view of life. I was impressed above all by the novels of Thomas Hardy. I think that it was his love of nature which first attracted me. I discovered in him the beauty of the English countryside, which I was now beginning to appreciate for myself, and so deeply did his description of it appeal to me that years later I made a walking tour of the Wessex country to follow out the path of the novels. But it was not only the beauty of it that attracted me; it was the sense of the interweaving of human destiny with the life of nature. I had always lived in the country but I had never really belonged to it. Hardy made me aware of the deep rhythm of peasant life in contact with the rhythm of nature, which I was discovering also in Wordsworth's poems like " Michael " and " The Leech Gatherer ".

At the same time, Hardy's sense of the tragedy of existence corresponded with my own deepest feelings. I had known nothing of tragedy in my own life, but I had begun to be aware that tragedy alone can reveal the deepest human values. I read Shakespeare in the light of Frank Harris's *The Man Shakespeare,* which with all its faults made Shakespeare intensely real to me, and of Middleton Murry's *Keats and Shakespeare.* I saw in the gradual development of Shakespeare's plays from the early comedies and histories, through the critical period of *Troilus and Cressida* and *Measure for Measure,* to the tragedies culminating in *King Lear,* what I felt was the most profound " criticism of life " (in Matthew Arnold's phrase), which had ever been made. By this time I was also able to read the Greek tragedians, and the sense that human life had never been lived so completely as in fifth century Athens, or portrayed with such clarity of vision as in the Tragedies of Aeschylus and Sophocles, became ingrained in me.

When, therefore, I read at the conclusion of Hardy's *Tess of the D'Urbervilles,* " The President of the Immortals (in Aeschylean phrase) had ended his sport with Tess ", this conception of God as a grim, impersonal power, to whom

human life is a kind of sport, fitted in with my general
view. I connected it with Shakespeare's despairing cry in
King Lear,

> *As flies to wanton boys are we to the gods,*
> *They kill us for their sport.*

But this did not incline me to atheism. I only felt that the
power behind the universe was an inscrutable mystery,
such as I had sensed in Conrad's descriptions of the sea and
the jungle.

In this way though I scarcely realised it my reading was
leading me to a view of life which was essentially pagan
rather than Christian. It is true that I revered the person
of Christ, but it was a Christ who was simply a perfect
human being like Socrates. One term when I was ill in the
infirmary with a poisoned knee, I read Giovanni Papini's
Story of Christ, and this filled me with a love of Christ as a
man which was never to leave me. I also read Tolstoi's
Kingdom of Heaven, the book in which he gives his own
interpretation of the Sermon on the Mount, and from this
time the Sermon on the Mount became the ideal of conduct for me; but it was the ideal of non-resistance to evil,
as Tolstoi understood it, which most attracted me. This
created such a strong conviction in me, that I joined with
three other friends in refusing to take rank as a lance-
corporal in the O.T.C.,* to which we were compelled to
belong.

It was during the period of the first Labour Government
in 1924, and we were ardent socialists and pacifists. Ram-
say MacDonald was our hero, and we were firmly convinced that nothing but militarism and imperialism stood
between the world and universal peace. These views were
not popular in the school, and we had some difficulty in
persuading the authorities of our sincerity. The headmaster, Mr Fyfe, however, showed his usual tact in hand-
ling the situation and eventually we were released from the
Corps altogether.

* Officers' Training Corps.

My socialism was partly due to the influence also of Bernard Shaw, whose plays were then at the height of their popularity. I took both the plays and the prefaces with intense seriousness. They formed, together with those of Ibsen and Galsworthy, a standard of criticism against the whole social order to which we belonged. It was, no doubt, partly no more than the rebellion of youth against the conventions of the past, but it was also part of a wider movement of revolt which had been released by the war and was to undermine the whole of our civilisation. I accepted not only Shaw's social criticism but also his view of Christianity. I remember that the Preface to *Androcles and the Lion* made a profound impression on me by its sceptical attitude towards Christianity. But it was Shaw's master, Samuel Butler, who shook my faith more than anybody. The tone and style of the *Notebooks* (I remember one of its headings, "Christ and the London and North Western Railway") fascinated me, and the suggestion in *The Way of all Flesh* that the narratives of the Resurrection in the four-Gospels could not be reconciled with one another, was as good as proof to me. I made no serious attempt to study the problems which were thus raised. It was rather that the whole course of my reading encouraged a sceptical attitude towards Christianity and there was nothing in my life which was sufficiently strong to stand against it.

We received, as I have said, no religious instruction, and I knew of no one who was capable of answering the questions which had been raised in my mind. I shared with all my contemporaries a prejudice against "dogma", that is to say, we did not believe in any authority beyond our own reason. In the same way we had a prejudice against "morality", that is, against any conception of an absolute moral law, which we were required to obey. We had our own code of behaviour, which forbade us to tell lies or to steal or to cheat, and there was a general convention against the expression of feeling or affection of any kind, which must have been the cause of a great deal of repression; but of the existence of a moral law or of the meaning of sin we had no notion.

My own feelings found their outlet mostly in poetry. My favourite poet to begin with was Swinburne, precisely because of the emotional effect which he produced upon me. It was the sound and rhythm of his poetry which I loved, and I was never tired of repeating the choruses from "Atalanta in Calydon" and the stanzas on the swallow in "Itylus". At the same time, though I did not take him very seriously, the shock to conventional morality contained in the Poems and Ballads certainly appealed to me, and I took pleasure in repeating the words of the "Hymn to Proserpine":

> *Thou hast conquered, O pale Galilaean,*
> *The world has grown grey from thy breath;*
> *We have drunken of things Lethaean,*
> *And fed on the fullness of death.*

Far more serious than the influence of Swinburne was that of Shelley. I had not read his *Necessity of Atheism*, and I should not have taken it very seriously if I had. But Shelley's poetry corresponded with all my deepest feelings. He had all the music and rhythm of Swinburne, but he had also a religious love of nature, which reflected my own awakening sense. His religion was, no doubt, pagan, but it was paganism founded not only on the Greek tragedians, but also on the philosophy of Plato, which I was learning to admire. Finally his political idealism and his conception of the regeneration of mankind in the "Prometheus Unbound" was for me, as it has been for so many others, a kind of substitute for the faith of the Gospel and the Apocalypse of St John.

Such were the different influences which had begun to shape my mind at the time when I experienced that kind of mystical exaltation in the presence of nature, which I have described, during my last term at school. This experience did not change the bent of my mind, but it gave it a new impulse. So far my inner life had been fed largely by my reading. Apart from this, I followed the routine of life at home and at school and was perfectly happy in it. I became captain of my house during my last year at school and won a scholarship at Oxford. This gave me more liberty and time to myself, and I obtained permission to give up playing games and spent my time in long rides and walks in the Sussex countryside. At home also I passed my days in walking in the woods and on the hills around Newbury. We had now moved to a little house on a common outside Newbury and there my new-found love for nature could have its full scope. I learned the names of all the birds and wild flowers of the neighbourhood, and would often spend whole days out on the hills or sitting by a stream in the woods and watching the wild life around me. This love of nature was very deep and had, as I have said, something of a religious character about it. I was seeking for something all the time, though I could hardly have said what it was. I liked the solitude and the silence of the woods and the hills. I felt there the sense of a Presence, something undefined and mysterious, which was reflected in the faces of the flowers and the movements of birds and animals, in the sunlight falling through the leaves and in the sound of running water, in the wind blowing on the hills and the wide expanse of earth and sky.

On my last day at school a friend and I walked out with knapsacks on our backs to explore the Sussex Downs. The action was in many ways symbolic, and marked out the course which my life was to follow. I was beginning to turn consciously to nature and to seek for a more primitive way of life than that of the modern world. I read Massingham's *Downland Man,* and with that and the background of Hardy's novels always in my mind, I had the sense of belonging to an immemorial past, in comparison with which modern civilisation was only a temporary excrescence. The long days spent tramping along the ancient tracks on the downs, with the larks singing in the air above

our heads and the harebells growing in the turf beneath
our feet; the contending with wind and rain and arriving
tired and footsore at an inn in the evening; the encounter
with people on the way, where conversation was so much
more free and easy than with people in the towns; all this
was an initiation into a new life for me. After that I could
never feel that I belonged to the modern industrial world
or settle down to a life of routine in a town. I felt like
Abraham·turning his back on Babylon, going out in search
of a country; but I was utterly ignorant of the nature of
the country which I was seeking, nor had I an inkling of the
vicissitudes I would have to suffer or of the renunciation
which I would have to make, before I would be able to set
my feet on the right path.

CHAPTER TWO

OXFORD

I went up to Oxford in October 1925 with a Classical Exhibition* to Magdalen College. The Exhibition was for fifty pounds a year, but the school made it up to one hundred pounds and Magdalen afterwards made it up to one hundred and fifty pounds, which was just sufficient to pay all my College expenses. For the rest, which was largely clothes and pocket money, I had to depend on my mother, and as we were still very poor, though the family income was beginning now to increase, I had to live as cheaply as possible.

Magdalen tended at that time to be divided into a group of comparatively rich young men, who lived in luxury and did little work, and a smaller group of scholars, who had to work hard and live cheaply. The balance is rather different now, but in those days I was often reminded of Chesterton's contemptuous description of Oxford as the playground of the idle rich. I was still a determined socialist, and one of my first acts was to join the Labour Club, and to help in the foundation of a Peace Union, which subsequently linked up with the No More War movement, and used to meet at the house of Mr and Mrs G. D. H. Cole. Socialism and pacifism were both growing strong in Oxford at that time, and one of my friends at school who had joined with me in opposition to the O.T.C., was elected the first Socialist Treasurer of the Union. He is now a Labour M.P. During the General Strike of 1926 we supported the miners and I offered to sell copies of the *Daily Worker* in the streets. I had studied the miners' case and was con-

* An Exhibition is a form of Scholarship, generally of less value than an actual Scholarship.

vinced of the justice of their cause, but I doubt whether I realised all the implications of the General Strike. However, the strike was called off before my services were required, and that was as far as I ever went towards political action.

My faith in socialism and in any form of political action soon declined, as I began to question the whole character of our civilisation. Spengler's *Decline of the West* was enjoying a great vogue at this time, and it gave me just the historical background which I needed to see our own civilisation in perspective. I saw that every civilisation in the past had its periods of rise and decline, and that our civilisation bore all the marks of decay. The great creative period of art and literature and of a vigorous social and political life was over, and we were living in an age comparable with that of the later Greek city-states and the Roman Empire, an age of demagogues and dictators, of bureaucracy and slave labour, of material luxury and sophistication. The publication of T. S. Eliot's *Waste Land* brought this home to me; in it one seemed to be listening to the death knell of our civilisation. The culture of the past which had once been an organic whole, now seemed to have been broken into fragments and reduced to chaos; and in *The Hollow Men* the disease of our civilisation appeared to be the prelude to the end of the world. The same impression of mental chaos and moral dissolution was given by James Joyce's *Ulysses*, which was then being passed round surreptitiously, as it was not allowed to be published in England. The parallel with the later Roman Empire, when there was the same failure of creative power and the same extension of material luxury with the sense of impending doom, seemed to be complete. In Oxford, though Logical Positivism had not yet arrived, the prevailing tone of thought was sceptical, and most of my friends who read philosophy soon came to the conclusion that truth was something which it was impossible to know.

I myself, after taking classical Honour Mods, decided,

instead of going on to Greats,* which would have meant reading some philosophy, to turn to English Literature. There were many reasons for this change. It was partly that I had little faith in philosophy, judging from the experience of my friends; but still more that I had begun to lose faith in intellect and reason altogether. I thought that intellectualism was the disease from which we were all suffering and which was bringing our civilisation to decay. My experience at school in the presence of nature seemed to be the one real thing in my life, to which I constantly returned; and I thought that the poetic imagination was the one means by which one could make contact with reality. By reading English Literature, therefore, I hoped that I would come nearer to the truth for which I was seeking than by any other means.

But my decision had other consequences which I did not foresee. I found that I was to have C. S. Lewis for my tutor. Lewis was at this time no more a Christian than I was, but he had been through the same phase of romanticism as I was then passing through, and had reached a more rational philosophy of life. I well remember my first meeting with him when I explained to him my reasons for reading English Literature. He protested vigorously against my view of life, but he was naturally unable to convince me, as I was not open to reason on the subject. I carried on a crusade against Dryden and Pope and the Age of Reason, which had an almost religious fervour in it. And indeed this was the only kind of religion which I acknowledged at this time. I had ceased to practise any form of Christianity, and I regarded Christianity as a religion of the past, which had ceased to have any significance for the present day.

I put forward this view in a paper which I read to a society over which Lewis presided at the time. I suggested

* " Honour Moderations " is the first part or preliminary, and " Greats " or " Literæ Humaniores ", the final school in the Classical Honours degree.

that we had to find a new religion and of this Wordsworth, Shelley and Keats, and the other leaders of the Romantic movement, were the prophets. The idea was not altogether so crude as it may sound. The religion of Wordsworth, as I found it expressed in the "Prelude" and in the "Lines Written Above Tintern Abbey", had a deeper meaning for me than anything else I had ever known, because it came nearer to my own experience. An abstract religion, which was all Christianity had ever been to me, can have little hold on us in comparison with one which corresponds with our own inner feelings. A time was to come when I would find that Christianity touched me more deeply than anything else, but at this time it was not so. The love of nature was the only thing which then moved me deeply, and I found in Wordsworth a religion which was wholly based on this. I thought especially of the lines:

> *For I have learned*
> *To look on nature not as in the hour*
> *Of thoughtless youth; but hearing oftentimes*
> *The still sad music of humanity,*
> *Not harsh nor grating, though of ample power*
> *To chasten and subdue. And I have felt*
> *A presence which disturbs me with the joy*
> *Of elevated thoughts; a sense sublime*
> *Of something far more deeply interfused,*
> *Whose dwelling is the light of setting suns,*
> *And the round ocean and the living air,*
> *And the blue sky, and in the mind of man:*
> *A motion and a spirit, that impels*
> *All thinking things, all objects of all thoughts,*
> *And rolls through all things.*

It was this spirit of nature which was the real object of my worship, and Wordsworth's description of it came to me with the force of a revelation. I doubt whether I was really a pantheist any more than Wordsworth was. It was simply that I was unable to relate this God of nature with anything which I had been taught in church. In the course of time I was to discover that the God who is manifested in nature is one and the same as the God who is preached in the Church, but at this time I could see no connection between them.

Even more precious to me than Wordsworth's conception of the nature of God was his description of the kind of trance which he experienced in the presence of nature, for this came even closer to my own experience.

> *Nor less I trust*
> *To them I may have owed another gift*
> *Of aspect more sublime; that blessed mood,*
> *In which the burthen of the mystery,*
> *In which the heavy and the weary weight*
> *Of all this unintelligible world*
> *Is lightened: that serene and blessed mood,*
> *In which the affections gently lead us on,*
> *Until, the breath of this corporeal frame*
> *And even the motion of our human blood*
> *Almost suspended, we are laid asleep*
> *In body and become a living soul:*
> *While with an eye made quiet with the power*
> *Of harmony, and the deep power of joy,*
> *We see into the life of things.*

Consciously or unconsciously it was this state of ecstasy, which I was seeking all the time, since I had first had a glimmer of it on that evening at school. It was in this state that I felt that wisdom was to be found, not in philosophy, nor in any form of religion, but in an experience which gave one a direct insight into the inner meaning of life. It was an emotional experience in which my whole being seemed to blend with the life of nature. I sought it continually, but though it came to me from time to time, it tended more and more to elude me. As time went on the sense of frustration which this engendered forced me to take another path, but for many years this was the inspiration and the goal of my life.

There is no doubt that there was a grave danger in this

cult of a peculiar emotional state, but I had developed it
into a deliberate philosophy. I considered that "thinking"
was the disease from which we were all suffering, so that we
were incapable of any spontaneous or creative action. The
mind moved continually round on itself so that it was
incapable of making contact with reality. I was prepared
to say with Keats, "O for a life of sensations rather than
of thoughts". I felt that it was through sensation rather
than through thought that one made contact with reality,
and that it was the imagination and not the reason, which
was the one power capable of interpreting sensation and
revealing its meaning. I took quite literally the saying of
Keats in the "Ode on a Grecian Urn", "Beauty is Truth,
Truth Beauty". It was through beauty, whether in nature
or in art, that I believed that one could make contact with
reality, and a form of truth which could not be expressed
in a form of beauty meant nothing to me. I conceived the
imagination, much as Wordsworth and Coleridge did, as
the faculty of truth; it was the means by which reality was
made present to the mind.

There was, of course, something one-sided in all this. I
was oblivious of every aspect of truth except that which
appealed to me. But at the same time I grasped a truth of
great importance. I had realised the danger of abstract
thought when it loses touch with the concrete realities of
life, and I had discovered that there is a truth of experience, which is mediated through the imagination, and
which often gives a deeper insight into reality than abstract
thought. "I believe," Keats had said, "in nothing but the
holiness of the heart's affections and the truth of the
imagination." This was the creed by which I wanted to
live, and I thought that reading English Literature would
bring me nearer to it than anything else.

My rooms during my second year at Magdalen were in
the eighteenth-century block called the New Buildings,
overlooking the medieval cloisters and the lovely fifteenth-
century tower. It was a perfect setting for the kind of life

which I wanted to live. There was a broad open space of lawn in front, with the deer park on one side and the river walks on the other. Outside my window there was an almond tree, which came into pink blossom early in the spring before any other colour had appeared, and in the river walks I could watch the procession of spring flowers coming out day by day from the snowdrops and crocuses at the end of January, followed by the small blue scylla and periwinkle in February, until the primroses and violets and daffodils came with March. There were nuthatches and tree-creepers and birds of all kinds nesting in the trees, and once I saw a kingfisher rise from the water just beneath me and fly into the sun, showing first the blood-red of its breast and then the blue glint of its wings. These walks by the river were the background to all my early years at Oxford, and I learned to love November and February above all other months for the air of mystery with which they clothed the misty landscape and the red-gold colour they brought out in the willow branches. In the summer months I would often take a punt out on the river all day, and do my reading for schools. I remember reading Spenser's *Faerie Queene* and Sir Philip Sidney's *Arcadia* in this way.

My two great friends at Magdalen, with whom I now began to share my life, were Hugh Waterman and Martyn Skinner. Hugh sat next to me one day at dinner in hall, and suddenly turned to me without any preface and said: "Do you like the letters of Keats?" This was sufficient introduction, and from that moment we became friends. Hugh shared all my feelings for nature and poetry, but he brought something more into my life. He had been at school at Marlborough, but he was never happy there, and his real life had always been at home. Here he was open to far more feminine influence than I had ever been, and he was altogether free from that habit of repressing all expression of affection from which I had suffered at school. He was naturally generous and affectionate, and was always full of consideration for others. I have known him empty his pockets when he met a poor man. It was his response to that sense of social injustice which we all felt in different ways. He brought a kind of grace into life which I had never experienced before. There was something in him of the spirit of St Francis of Assisi. He always had flowers in his room, and a copy of Botticelli's "Primavera" on his walls, and he and Martyn had between them records of almost all Beethoven's symphonies and the last quartets.

Hugh wrote a good deal of romantic poetry at this time, but it was Martyn who was to become a serious poet. He had been at school at Clifton, and had made himself unpopular by writing satirical verse in the style of Pope; but under Hugh's influence he began to write a long romantic poem in the style of Keats's "Endymion". Later he was to achieve a perfect mastery of the heroic couplet, as an instrument alike of wit and satire and of a sensitive feeling for nature, in the *Letters to Malaya,* which won him the Hawthornden Prize in 1943. He soon became devoted also to Malory's *Morte d'Arthur,** which expressed for us all the sense of the beauty and the chivalry of the past which seemed to have departed from the modern world. Martyn felt more keenly than any of us the conflict between the ugliness of the modern industrial city and the ideal of a life in harmony with nature which we all desired. It was as evident in Oxford as anywhere, where the old university town and the once beautiful countryside were being slowly submerged by the modern city spreading out from Cowley on one side, and covering the fields of North Oxford with suburbs on another. It was not so much the poverty of the industrial workers which troubled me now, as the sense that human life was being impoverished and degraded by being deprived of that beauty which belonged to it by right. This was the problem which faced us now,

* He has recently (1964) finished the concluding volume of a "satiric epic", the first part of which, *Merlin*, was published by Chapman & Hall 1952, and the second two parts, *The Return of Arthur*, 1 and 2, 1955 and 1959.

and in our efforts to solve it, we were to be driven to make
an experiment which was to change the whole course of our
lives.

Our first reaction to this situation was that of flight. We
escaped whenever it was possible from Oxford into the
surrounding country, to the Cotswolds, the Chilterns and
the Berkshire Downs. There was an obvious inconsistency
in this, as we were dependent on a car for our escape, and
we carried the marks of the Industrial Revolution with us
wherever we went. A time was to come when we were to
make a serious attempt to face this inconsistency, but at
first we were scarcely aware of it. There was an added
irony in the fact that Martyn's father, Sir Sydney Skinner,
was the Chairman of Barkers and had been largely responsible for building up that model of modern commercialism
which stood for all that we detested.

But however much inconsistency there might be in our
actual circumstances, we tried to work out a consistent
theory to direct our lives. We thought that the source of all
the evil to which we were opposed was to be found in the
scientific mind. I do not think that we should ever have
condemned either science or reason in themselves. It was
the divorce of the scientific and rational mind from nature,
from the world of instinct and feeling and imagination
which seemed to us to be the root of all evil. It was when
the human mind became separated from its roots in feeling
and instinct that it became diseased, and the infallible mark
of the disease was the ugliness of its productions. This was
how we explained the ugliness of the modern city in comparison with the beauty of the Cotswold towns and villages
which we visited. When the mind was in harmony with
nature, as it had been in the past, then its products had a
spontaneous beauty, which flowed from men's hands with
the same certainty as ugliness passed from the machine into
its products. The Cotswold village or church or farmhouse
was possessed of an infallible beauty, whether it was of the
fourteenth, the sixteenth or the eighteenth century, just as

the nineteenth century town or house or factory was possessed by ugliness. The one seemed to have grown out of
the hills in which it was set by a natural process, and hand
and brain of man working in harmony with nature according to her own intrinsic laws : the other was imposed on
the countryside without relation to its features or character.

This contrast became most strikingly clear to us when,
after we had finished our time at Oxford, we went for a
motor tour, starting from Cambridge and going up through
Peterborough to Lincoln and York. Even at Cambridge
we could not but be struck by the beauty of the town which
had kept its character of a university town while Oxford
had become commercialised. But it was at Peterborough
that the full contrast dawned upon my mind. I shall never
forget the sight of the great cathedral rising above the
hideous smoky city like an apparition from another world.
It was literally as though they belonged to a different world
and sprang from a different race of men. When we went
on to Lincoln and York and spent days at each place studying the sculpture of the capitals and the Angel choir, and
the stained glass of York Minster and the other churches of
York, we seemed to see the evidence for another Fall of
Man. Here we seemed to be in the presence of an unfallen
world, where men were possessed of a sense of beauty which
had since been suddenly and calamitously lost. That there
was something more than a sense of beauty which had
been lost; that there was also a sense of values, of something sublime and beyond the reach of modern man, I
think we may have dimly discerned, but it was the beauty
of it which filled us with such astonishment and awe.

From York we went on to the Lake District and spent a
fortnight at Ullswater. Here an experience of another kind
awaited us, but it was no less imposing. Wordsworth was
one who had stood at the very turn of the tide, when the
Industrial Revolution was just beginning. He had consciously and deliberately turned to the primitive simplicity
of his home among the hills and streams of the Lake Dis-

trict for the inspiration both of his religion and of his poetry. It was the same for us. We felt that here among these hills we could find that communion with nature in which the source of all beauty was to be found. I remember that I went out once alone among the hills, when a mist began to gather, and I felt myself alone in that mysterious solitude, as though I had been at the bottom of the sea, cut off from all the haunts of men; and once again the sense of that Presence which I had experienced at school took possession of me. But such experiences were never more than transitory. Our lives were too unstable for them to be anything else. We did not belong like Wordsworth to the Lakes. We did not belong anywhere. That was part of our misery; whether we liked it or not, we were uprooted like the rest of the world, and wherever we went we could not escape ourselves.

Nevertheless we went everywhere we could in search of solitude. One year we camped on the west coast of Ireland, on a cliff in West Kerry, a few yards from the Atlantic with nothing between ourselves and America. It was perhaps the wildest and most primitive place which we ever found. There were one or two cottages around, where we were warmly welcomed and where we got our bread and milk. We had to fetch our bacon and other stores from Bally-ferriter, a small village about six miles away. Otherwise we were undisturbed, except for the sea-birds which were crying all day over the sea before us. There were gulls of all sorts, and sometimes we would see a gannet diving from a height to spear a fish in the sea, or a cormorant would fly out from a ledge among the rocks where they congregated. On our walks we would sometimes come upon a flock of two or three hundred curlews, which would fly off with their wild, eerie cries. We had a wide plain behind us going back to the Brandon mountains with scarcely a tree to be seen on it, so violent was the wind there. The Atlantic rollers would sometimes toss their spray seventy feet high over the cliffs, which made us feel the savage fury of the elements.

We would generally go out alone each day and find some place where we could sit in solitude, and read or write or just meditate. Some of us were interested in Celtic lore and mythology, but for the most part it was just the presence of wild nature which we sought and the sense of being alone between the hills and the sky and the sea. It would be difficult to define exactly what we were seeking but I think that in an obscure way without knowing it we were seeking God.

Among ourselves we still thought in terms of the imagination. This was the faculty which was the source of all creative power : and it was to awaken this power in ourselves that we sought above all other things. This was the power which we felt was being destroyed by modern industrialism and which alone could save the world. We thought of it still, I think, in terms of Keats, but it was the Keats of the later version of " Hyperion ", who had learned that he must leave behind him the beauty of the senses and the emotions, which had held him captive, and discover the beauty which comes from suffering which has been accepted. I do not think that we were at all capable as yet of accepting suffering in any form for ourselves, but we recognised that there was a beauty which came out of suffering, which was above all other beauty. The last plays of Shakespeare (*Cymbeline, The Winter's Tale,* and *The Tempest*) when he had passed through the storm of the Tragedies and emerged into a new vision of life : the last Quartets of Beethoven, where he seemed to have passed beyond all human emotion into a world where pain and joy are reconciled : these were the inspiration of our lives.

It was the time when the tales of Tchekov were being admired and studied, especially by Mr Middleton Murry, who had been our guide for so long, and we found in them that calm, dispassionate facing the tragedy of life which we felt to be the ideal. We resented any attempt to pass judgment, especially any kind of moral judgment. The perfect man was the man, who, like Shakespeare in Keats's phrase, "had no identity": who mirrored life in all its phases of comedy and tragedy and entered into each human character without imposing his own "identity" upon it. To feel all the force of evil, to let it sweep over one and enter into the very depths of one's being and to conquer it by not resisting it: this seemed to us the height of perfection, and this is what we felt had been realised in the death of Christ. We did not believe in the Resurrection, but we thought that, simply by suffering evil as he had done without resistance, he had in a mysterious way overcome it: that his death had given meaning to life just as in their own way Shakespeare and Beethoven had given a new meaning to life. We were still very far from accepting this in our own life and conduct but I think that this represents our thought at this time. We accepted Keats's idea of "dying into life" as the expression of that mystery, which underlay all great poetry and all great art, but we were far from realising its implications in our own lives. It is characteristic that we never gave a thought to what might be the religion of the Irish peasants who received us so kindly and whom we so much admired. We were only interested in finding remnants of Celtic folklore among them.

Perhaps what kept us from orthodox Christianity more than anything else was our attitude towards morality. Just as we saw in the scientific mind, with its lack of imagination, the cause of the ugliness and inhumanity of modern civilisation, so we looked on law and morality, in so far as they were separated from love, as the principal cause of evil. I do not think that we should have condemned law and morality as such, any more than we condemned science and reason in themselves; but the divorce of the moral reason and conscience from instinct and passion was what we rebelled against. Love was for us in the sphere of action what imagination was in the world of thought and production. Reason without imagination and morality without love were the two great sources of evil in human life and in our own civilisation in particular.

In this view we were no doubt following in the steps of Blake and of the whole of that tradition of protest against the Puritanism of our ancestors which has gradually won its victory in the modern world. We based ourselves consciously on the teaching and example of Christ. We saw that it was not the Publicans and sinners, but the Scribes and Pharisees, the representatives of religion, law and morality in their strictest form, who had crucified Christ. As a result we tended to identify all organised religion and especially all clergy with the Scribes and Pharisees and to regard them as the natural enemies of the Gospel. At a later date the study of St Paul's teaching of the relation between the Law and the Gospel was to change my view of this and to provide a solution to the problem. But the paradox remains at the heart of Christianity and the problem which it raises is one which every generation and every individual has to face.

At this time after the Great War, at Oxford the reaction against conventional morality was so strong that it was difficult not to be submerged by it. Just as most people came to the conclusion that there was no certain truth which could be known in philosophy, so I think the majority came to think that there was no moral law that had any authority. To be free to develop one's capacities and to express one's nature was all that was required. Certainly we did not believe in Original Sin and there was a general tendency to regard human nature as intrinsically good and only in need of education in order to be perfect. Above all, we believed that there was no aspect of life which should be shirked and that one should be prepared to know everything.

I myself had begun to read French novels when I was at school, and later during one of the vacations at Oxford my brother took me to Paris where we did the round of the cabarets and music halls of Montmartre. But I don't think that it was so much that immorality attracted me as that I wanted to know what was to be known and to learn to face it, like the novelist who can only describe a scene of passion when he has learned to look on it with detachment. It was no doubt a dangerous course to follow and I was still utterly ignorant of myself; but it forced me to face the problem of the true nature of love.

In this I was helped by the writings of D. H. Lawrence, to which I was introduced by another friend at this time, Hugh l'Anson Fausset. My family were then living in the little cottage outside Newbury which I have mentioned, and Fausset's house was only five minutes' walk away. We met first at a tennis party, where we found ourselves sitting out together, and entered into conversation. That conversation continued all that evening at his house, and was the beginning of endless talks and of a friendship which has never been broken. He was several years older than I was and had been reviewing books for some time for *The Times Literary Supplement*. He was also engaged on a series of books on Keats, Shelley, Wordsworth and Coleridge, in which he subjected Romanticism to a far deeper criticism than I was able to do. Later in his studies of Donne and Tolstoy he was to analyse the split in the modern mind which took place at the Renaissance and reached its culmination in the Russia of Tolstoy and Dostoevsky. He lent me Lawrence's *Fantasia of the Unconscious* and some of his novels and stories, and I began to see more clearly into the cause of the disease of modern civilisation.

I think that this was my first introduction to the idea of the unconscious, and it was not until many years later that I was to find a complete analysis of this idea in the psychology of Jung. But Lawrence revealed to me the nature of the conscious mind and its rational processes on the one side and the unconscious soul with its deep instinctive feelings and its power of intuition on the other. I saw now that the disease was not only in our civilisation as a whole but in myself. I had been living all through my life at school and at Oxford on my conscious mind and the unconscious life of instinct had been habitually repressed. My awakening to the beauty of nature and my feeling for poetry had come as a merciful release for this repression, but it had still left me unbalanced. In particular Lawrence revealed to me the power of sex as one of the two poles of our being which can only be suppressed at the risk of destruction.

I do not think that I ever derived from Lawrence the idea that the cure for all our troubles was simply sexual indulgence, though that was the general view. On the contrary, he taught me what I believe is the only true solution to the problem, namely that sex is essentially a " holy " instinct. It is not merely good in itself (this we were all prepared to admit), but it is something "sacred". The evil of immorality in sex is not merely that of self-indulgence, but the profanation of something sacred, the desecration of a holy instinct which arises from the depths of our unconscious being and is the bearer of life or death. I think that Lawrence first made me begin to see that the evil of our civilisation lay in this, that it had desecrated the sources of life. Primitive man might often be immoral and cruel and superstitious, but he retained a sense of the "holy"; he was still in contact with the inner sources of life, and therefore there were beauty and dignity in his life. We with all our science and reason and morality had lost this sense of the "holy" and therefore all our works were ugly and our minds were sterile.

Later I found support for this view in the novels of Tolstoy. When I read in *Anna Karenina* of Levin leaving his life in town and in society to go and work among the peasants on his farm in the country, I saw that Tolstoy was trying to face the same situation as we were. In Russia the conflict between the civilisation of Moscow and St Petersburg and the life of the peasants in the villages was far more intense than in England, but it only focused the same problem more clearly. In Russia the social life of the towns was felt as a foreign importation and the life of the peasants was tragically poor, only just emerging from serfdom; but still the life of the peasants retained something of its ancient "holy" character, which Tolstoy felt in the depths of his being; while the social life of the towns seemed a superficial mockery. It is difficult to say how long these ideas were developing in my mind, but I think that they had already taken root towards the end of my time at Oxford.

More and more we spent our time during the vacations on a farm in the Cotswolds, where we felt nearer to the rhythm of nature and where we made friends with the country people. The prospect of earning a living by working in a town became almost unendurable, and at the time I saw no hope of any employment except as a schoolmaster.

But before I had to face this prospect seriously, we came to a decision which was to change the whole course of our lives. Oxford had left us with no definite religion or philosophy of life and with a profound sense of discontent with the world in which we were compelled to live. But not only were we disturbed in mind : we had also begun to suffer physically from the conflict with life in which we were engaged. Hugh had a serious illness, and both Martyn and I suffered from different complaints, which were partly psychological (at least so it appears to me now) in their origin. We felt that we must do something to recover our balance and to enable us to come to grips with the problem of life. So far we had only been playing at it. We had stayed for months on a farm but we had never attempted to do any work there. We had always been lookers on, making friends with the country people but never sharing their life. Now we decided that we would try to live this life in earnest. We would buy a cottage in one of these Cotswold villages and try to live in the utmost simplicity, supporting ourselves as far as possible by our own labour. Both Hugh and Martyn had money of their own, and though I had none, it was decided that we would have everything in common and share a common account. At the same time, our minds began to undergo a transformation. We began to discard our romanticism and to give ourselves to more serious study and thought.

CHAPTER THREE

PHILOSOPHY

When I came down from Oxford, C. S. Lewis advised me to read some philosophy to make up for my not having read Greats. As is often the way with a tutor at Oxford, our relationship had gradually been transformed into one of friendship, which was cemented by our going for a walking tour together with a friend shortly afterwards.

Lewis had the most exact and penetrating mind I had ever encountered, and his criticism of the essays which I brought to him each week when I was reading English Literature was the best education which I could have had. He had always a complete mastery of the subject, and never allowed any looseness of thought or expression. But these criticisms often led on to a general discussion, which was sometimes continued almost to midnight, and we began now to think along almost identical lines.

While I was reading philosophy I kept up a constant correspondence with him, and it was through him that my mind was gradually brought back to Christianity. During the following years we pursued the study of Christianity together, and first one of us and then the other would make the discovery of some masterpiece of Christian thought which we had not known before. I remember in particular how the discovery of William Law's *Serious Call* and Butler's *Analogy of Religion* excited us both. An unseen hand seemed to be leading us both to the same goal. Our ways were to part in the end, but I owe to his friendship more than I can say, and no differences which later arose between us were able to disturb it. We had learned to recognise the value of what we held in common and neither of us could ever forget the miracle of grace which changed us from pagans into Christians.

I started philosophy with Descartes's *Meditations* and *Discourse of Method*. Descartes had no great attraction for me, but I liked his easy style as of a man of the world and his way of making a clean sweep of everything which had gone before, and beginning to think out everything afresh. I was not interested in systems and dogmas; I wanted to find a philosophy by which I could live, and I found in Descartes's earnest effort to think out everything for himself a genuine inspiration. I do not think that I was much impressed with his proof of the existence of God, but the idea that the existence of God was capable of philosophical proof was new to me, and must have affected me accordingly. In the same way, I am sure that I did not realise the implications of his theory that the mind and the body are two perfectly separate substances; otherwise I might have seen in his philosophy the source of that split in the human consciousness of which I had been made aware. The idea that the mind was a pure spirit and the body a pure mechanism was surely the most disastrous error ever propagated, which was to put philosophy on a false trail for centuries and to vitiate all modern thought.

But I did not linger long enough over Descartes to discover it. I went on from him to Spinoza, and there I discovered a philosopher after my own heart. Even now I cannot forget the intense excitement with which Spinoza filled me. There was first of all the incitement of the noble preface to the *Ethics* in which he declared how having considered that neither wealth nor fame nor honour were of any value in comparison with wisdom, he determined to devote his life to the pursuit of wisdom. I had already learned something of this love of wisdom from Socrates, but Spinoza brought it nearer home to me and made it seem accessible as a goal in my own life. It might have been thought that Spinoza's rigidly mathematical style, treating every problem in philosophy like a problem in geometry, would have antagonised me. But perhaps I was already sufficiently in revolt against my romanticism to want a

dose of pure reason; perhaps also the economy of Spinoza's
style with its clarity and precision gave me a kind of
æsthetic pleasure such as I was later to find in the style of
St Thomas Aquinas. But what really touched me deeply was
the moral earnestness of Spinoza. It was the sense that here
was a man who was seeking with his whole strength for a
solution to the problem of life, and whose enthusiasm made
itself felt through the bare structure of his thought. I was
particularly impressed with his analysis of the emotions,
and with the idea that it is by gaining an "adequate idea"
of our emotions that we are able to be free from their
control. This was the idea of which I had been in search
before. I saw that it was only by self-knowledge that one
could learn self-control. It was not by running away from
one's passions or by trying to suppress them that one could
be free from their power: it was by learning to face them,
to study them and know their source and their direction.
I think that I assumed too easily that to know one's nature
was to be able to control it, but it was a valuable lesson
nonetheless.

Spinoza's idea of God impressed me with its logical consistency, though I do not think that I took very seriously
his idea that extension is an attribute of God no less than
thought. But his conception of the "intellectual love of
God" in the last book of the *Ethics* was of incalculable
significance to me. I think that it taught me for the first
time to think rationally about God. My rebellion in the
past had not been so much against a God of reason as
against a phantom of my imagination. We all of us grow
up with some more or less fantastic idea of God which we
inherit from childhood, and it is against this phantom of the
imagination that we rebel as our reason begins to develop.
My experience at school had made me aware of a deeper
reality behind the face of nature, but it had been no
more than a confused intuition; I had never subjected it
to a rational scrutiny. This was what Spinoza did for me.
He showed me that the power behind the universe was a

rational power, and that to know this reason of the universe was man's highest wisdom.

But more than this. This reason of the universe could not only be known but also loved. To accept the order of the universe with one's will; to identify oneself with the will of God was the source of all happiness. It is true that all men must infallibly obey the will of God because the universe is subject to a law of absolute necessity; but we were free to choose whether we should obey willingly or unwillingly. There are some to whom this will seem a harsh creed, but to me its logical consistency had an immense fascination. It corresponded with all I had learned to believe about the acceptance of the tragedy of life, as I saw it in Shakespeare and Beethoven.

I had, moreover, begun to read the *Meditations* of Marcus Aurelius at this time, and I found in them an almost identical philosophy of life expressed with a more personal charm and no less nobility of character. I shall never forget how the "piety" of Marcus Aurelius touched me, his deep reverence for nature and for the order of the universe, which he expressed in the words, " Shall one say of Athens, O beautiful City of Cecrops, and shall not I say of the world, O beautiful City of God?" His conception of nature as one vast organism in which each element had to play its part and in which each individual human life was but one element, appealed both to my imagination and my reason. It offered an explanation of the problem of evil, which was closely akin to that of Spinoza, that the cause of suffering was that each individual could not see his place in the pattern of the whole and thereby put himself in conflict with it; but if he could learn by reason to know his place within the whole, and deliberately accept it, then though he might suffer in his feelings his mind would be at peace. No less appealing was the idea that virtue was not something which required a reward, but that it was its own reward. To be virtuous was to live according to the reason, the law of the universe, of which our own reason was a part, and a virtuous act was simply an action which was " according to nature " like the growth of fruit on a tree.

My first reading in philosophy therefore only came to confirm and to give a rational basis to what I had already come to believe. But my next step was to take me much further. I began to read Berkeley's *Principles of Human Knowledge*. I was charmed first of all by Berkeley's style, for I still read very definitely with an eye to the literary quality of what I was studying. Berkeley's prose belongs to that Golden Age of English prose when the magnificent elaborations of Sir Thomas Browne were abandoned for the simple, direct and energetic style of Dryden, Swift and Defoe. It was a perfect instrument of philosophic thought and no one was a greater master of it than Berkeley. But it was not only the style, it was also the thought that charmed me. When I read : " Some truths there are so near and obvious to the mind that a man need only open his mind to perceive them. Such I take this important one to be : *viz.* that all the choir of heaven and all the furniture of the earth, in a word all the bodies which compose the mighty frame of the world, have not any subsistence without a mind, that their being is to be perceived and known; that consequently so long as they are not actually perceived by me or do not exist in my mind or that of any other created spirit, they must either have no existence at all or else subsist in the mind of some eternal Spirit ", I felt that a new light had dawned for me. It was not that I was for a moment taken in by the idea that the existence of things depends on our observation of them, but that I saw quite clearly that it was absolutely impossible to conceive of things existing without a mind to know them, that things were essentially ideas, ideas not of our minds but of that universal mind or Spirit of the universe of which I had learned from Spinoza and Marcus Aurelius. But there was now no question of confusing the universe and God as Spinoza had done by claiming that extension was an attribute of God. God was a mind, a pure Spirit, and the uni-

verse was the thought of his mind, while our own perception of things was simply a limited participation, as Marcus
Aurelius had held, in the mind or reason of God.

But this theory had a further significance for me in that
its author was a Bishop of the Established Church. This
was the first time that it had occurred to me that the doctrine of the Church had any rational justification. I felt
that this eternal Spirit of Berkeley was one with that Presence which I had experienced in nature and now for the
first time I perceived that it might have some relation with
the God of Christian orthodoxy. This was a momentous
event in my life. I knew that Berkeley had a mind immeasurably superior to that of Shaw or Samuel Butler or
anyone whose opinion I had accepted in the past, and I
conceived a new respect for orthodoxy. I was, of course, very
far from accepting orthodox doctrine, but from this time
my mind began to be open to it as it had not been before.

This was confirmed by the next reading which I under-
took. I did not delay over Hobbes, Locke and Hume:
neither Hobbes' materialism nor Locke's common-sense
philosophy nor Hume's scepticism would have had anything to give me. But I made a serious effort to read
Kant's *Critique of Pure Reason*. I accepted immediately
his refutation of Hume's scepticism, by showing that there
are certain truths which the mind cannot doubt, such as the
truths of number, like seven and five is twelve, or truths of
logic, like " the part cannot be greater than the whole ".
This evidence that the human mind finds within itself
certain principles which cannot be doubted and which are
the source of all scientific knowledge was of great value. I
was taken also with his distinction between the world as it
appears to the senses, the " phenomenal world ", and the
world as it appears to the understanding, the " noumenal
world " : but I do not think that I ever accepted his view
that our knowledge in either case depends on the structure
of our own minds and tells us nothing of reality as it is.

In this I was helped by reading two books by Coleridge,

which Lewis recommended to me at this time, the *Aids to Reflection* and *The Friend*. These books are not very widely read, but they are the work of one of the most universal minds in English literature, written at the end of his life when he had mastered all the new German philosophy and created a new synthesis from it. Coleridge's life was, of course, a tragedy, and he never developed his full powers either as a poet or as a philosopher; but these are still the work of a great and original mind, and one which was endeared to me by long familiarity. I read them with profound attention and they had a remarkable effect on my mind. In the first place, I again found a great thinker who employed all his powers as a philosopher in defence of orthodox Christianity. But in the second place I found a synthesis between the philosophy of Kant and that Platonic philosophy which had attracted me from my earliest years. Coleridge accepted Kant's distinction between the phenomenal and the noumenal world, but he related the noumenal world to Plato's world of ideas. What existed as ideal in the human mind existed as law in nature : there was a real correspondence between the mind and nature. The illusion that the human mind can never do more than contemplate its own ideas, which had beguiled philosophers from the time of Descartes was therefore overcome.

But Coleridge went further than this; he related both the forms which exist in nature and the ideas which exist in the human mind to their source in the mind of God. Both forms and ideas are but reflections or copies of the eternal ideas which exist in the mind of God and give to all things the reality which they possess. Thus Coleridge opened my mind to the full scope of that Platonic philosophy which I had dimly felt to contain the explanation of nature which I needed when I was reading Shelley. But with Plato himself there had always been the difficulty that he had never seemed to distinguish clearly between the human concept of a thing and the " idea " which is the source of its reality : and when in the *Republic* I found Plato excluding the poets from his ideal state because they did not deal with reality but only with the " copy of a copy ", I felt outraged. To me it was clear that the poet was often nearer to the reality than the philosopher, because he sought to embody reality, that is truth itself, in an image which was a living symbol of reality and made it present to our souls in a manner which the abstract concepts of the philosopher could never do.

This problem of the relation between the poet and the philosopher in respect of truth was to puzzle me for many years, but Coleridge really supplied the answer, as, being both poet and philosopher, he was well qualified to do. Both poet and philosopher " imitate " the truth, that is, the pure idea which alone is absolute truth and equally (as Keats had seen) absolute beauty. The philosopher represents it in a concept which expresses its essence deprived of all those accidental elements with which it is clothed in reality. But the poet represents it in an image, which is concrete not abstract, and clothed in all the richness of sensual and emotional colouring which belong to it in reality. So, for example, the philosopher like Aristotle tells us that man is a "rational animal". This gives us the essence of man and is of incalculable value in any attempt to form a scientific idea of the nature of man. But the poet like Shakespeare gives us, in Hamlet or in Lear, man in the concrete; an individual man with all the accidents of his personality, but at the same time an image of universal man, of our human nature as we all recognise it to be under all its different appearances. This was, however, a view at which I only arrived after many years of struggling with the problem; but I think that it would be true to say that Coleridge in the *Aids to Reflection* and *The Friend* and also in the magnificent chapter on the imagination in *Biographia Literaria* gave me the lines of a true answer. And this was not merely a speculative problem, because all the time I was concerned with the problem in my own life of reconciling reason and imagination.

In all my reading I was seeking, perhaps only half consciously, to find rational evidence for the existence of that which I had experienced in the presence of nature at school and at Oxford. It was the experience which came first and so it must always be. All our knowledge comes to us directly or indirectly from experience, from the vital experience of the senses and the imagination. The philosopher can interpret our experience in the light of those principles with which Kant had shown me the human mind is endowed, but ideas can never take the place of experience. An idea of God which had no relation to my own experience would have had no interest for me. It was because I found in Berkeley and Spinoza and Kant a rational explanation of what I had begun to learn from my own experience that it came to me with such force of conviction.

But at the same time I was becoming more and more aware of the limitations of my own experience. I still spent all my spare time in long solitary walks in the country among the woods and commons and on the downs, which lay within walking distance of my home outside Newbury. But it was no longer the face of nature which seemed to contain the meaning of life for me. I felt now that the real mystery lay within. Spinoza's *Ethics* and the *Meditations* of Marcus Aurelius had awakened this sense within me of a moral life, in which the real meaning of life was to be found. But this moral life was not merely a life of reason and of speculation, it was something which involved one's whole being. I began to see moral virtue as the flowering of one's whole nature. The Beatitudes had always had for me an immense attraction, and now I began to see the whole life of virtue as something irresistibly attractive. It was a kind of imaginative idealism in which my feelings were deeply engaged. It was, of course, still very far from real virtue because my will had hardly begun to be trained, but it acted as an intense incitement. Above all it made it impossible for me to look on philosophy as merely an exercise of the speculative reason. It was a matter of passionate interest which I felt to hold the meaning of life for me. No doubt this often made my reading defective from a rational point of view, but it prevented it from becoming an academic exercise and made it a profound personal experience.

This was still more clearly true of the two books which now engaged my attention, the *Confessions* of St Augustine and the *Divine Comedy* of Dante. I read both of these primarily for their literary interest. I think that it was when I was just going to read the *Confessions* that I mentioned the fact to C. S. Lewis in the course of a conversation, and he said, as though it were a matter of course : " Of course, you will read it in the original." As a matter of fact, I had had no intention of doing so, but I immediately felt his words as a challenge and replied : " Yes." From that time I made a point of always reading in the original language if I was able, and I have always been grateful for this experience. Even if one's knowledge of the language were imperfect, it gave one a sense of being in contact with the mind of the author as no translation can do. The mere mental effort was a stimulus and this made the contact the more vivid. The result of this was that each book became a living contact with the mind of a man, who was often more real to me than the people with whom I was living.

It was so that the splendour of St Augustine's *Confessions* broke upon me. I do not think that I took in a tithe of their meaning, but the sense of contact with a mind, which was consumed with an ardour for truth and for that life of virtue which I desired, penetrated into the depths of my soul. It was an experience which I can only compare to the ardour with which I used to read Shelley and Swinburne. But the emotion which it excited in me was no longer the vague emotionalism of Swinburne, but a passion of religious love of an intensity which I had never known before. But at the same time it was an " intellectual love " like that of Spinoza, governed by an intelligence as clear and keen as his, and not blurred like that of Shelley by an undisciplined imagination. Here was, in fact, what I had so long desired to find, a record of a personal experience of passionate intensity and immense imaginative power, engaging all the energies of the intellect and the will in the search for truth. From this time truth could never be for me anything less than this, something which corresponded to the needs of one's whole being and called forth all the energies of one's nature.

How much St Augustine's thought actually penetrated my mind, I would not like to say, but once again as with Berkeley I could not but be aware that here was a great Christian, whose idea of God was both as real and as rational as I could wish. I know that the invocation of the fourth chapter made a deep impression on me. " O thou supreme, most powerful, most merciful, most just, most secret, most present, most beautiful, most mighty; most constant, and incomprehensible, immutable and yet changing all things; never new and never old, yet renewing all things, and drawing such as are proud into decay though they know it not. Ever in action and ever quiet; heaping up yet needing nothing, upholding, filling and protecting, creating, nourishing and perfecting all things." It was not that I fully grasped this conception of God, but that it presented itself to my mind as something rich and deep and full of meaning and demanding all one's powers to understand it.

In the same way St Augustine's interpretation of the Bible, especially in the last three books, fascinated me as revealing a depth of meaning which had never even occurred to me, and at the same time as showing a range of intelligence which made the criticisms of modern sceptics seem childish. I had not begun to study the questions which were raised but I felt it as something which lay before me, and my mind was at least open to orthodoxy. I think that it was also in St Augustine that I first heard of the " Catholic Church " as a reality which commanded respect and demanded investigation. I must still have had the vaguest idea of what it signified, but it at least appeared now on the map of life for me, though it was a long time before it was anything more than an idea in a book. I was still far from being a Christian even in name, and I think that I still regarded Christianity as a thing of the past. It interested me as a historical phenomenon and I was prepared to give it serious attention; but St Augustine took his place in my mind along with Marcus Aurelius and Spinoza, and I felt no more called on to be a Christian than to be a Jew or an ancient Roman.

This was the spirit in which I began to read Dante. I approached him as I had done Homer and Virgil and Milton as a poet, whose religion was of no more importance than the Pagan gods of Homer or Virgil's glorification of Augustus and Roman Imperialism. Dante's descent into hell had its antecedent in the descent of Aeneas into the underworld, and the whole background of Hell and Purgatory and Paradise was a piece of mythology such as I had always considered that of *Paradise Lost*. My reading of Dante was nevertheless a turning point in my life. In the first place, simply as a poet he seemed to me to be above everyone that I had ever read. I began to read him in the Temple Classics edition with the Italian text on one side and a very exact and scholarly translation on the other, but I soon found that I could do without the translation and could enjoy it as poetry. In pure sound, which was still my first attraction in poetry, I suppose that no lovelier language than the Italian of Dante has ever been known. But with this there was also an intensity of feeling and a richness and at the same time precision of imagery beyond anything in the Romantic poets. Dante therefore answered all my requirements in poetry up to that time, but he also gave me something more, a "criticism of life" on a level which was deeper than that of Shakespeare. When I found Paolo and Francesca placed in Dante's hell, my view of romantic love was radically changed. For Paolo and Francesca had done nothing but surrender to that passion of love which I had been taught to regard as the greatest good in life. They had done what Romeo and Juliet and Antony and Cleopatra and all the heroes and heroines in fiction had been admired for doing, and their punishment was simply to be consumed eternally in the fire of their passion. This was not the judgment, moreover, of a Puritan moralist like Milton, but of one who had felt the passion of love to its depths.

In the past, my objection to "morality" had been that it seemed to be a denial of life. .It set up cold reason against the fire of life, and I felt like Aucassin and Nicolette, the lovers in the medieval tale, that it was better to go to hell with the great lovers than to go to heaven with the moralists. But now Dante showed me that it was not the fire of love which was evil but the passion which made one its slave. A passion which was disciplined and controlled was stronger and deeper than an undisciplined love. I had already begun to glimpse this in Spinoza, but Dante presented it to me with all the force of great poetry. It was clear to me that the strength of Dante in comparison with poets like Shelley and Keats lay in the greater moral and intellectual power of his mind. He was a greater poet because he was a greater lover than they; with him the moral and intellectual power came to reinforce the power of love and not to destroy it. This was a lesson of enormous importance which it was to take me years to assimilate.

Its importance to me at the time can be seen in the fact that it was not the *Inferno* or the *Paradiso* which affected me most deeply but the *Purgatorio*. It is well known that Dante's journey through hell and purgatory to Paradise was intended among other things as an allegory of the soul's journey through the purgative and the illuminative way to the state of union with God. Of this I had very little conception at the time, but the reading of the *Purgatorio* acted nevertheless as a real illumination of my mind. It was not merely a poetic experience but a moral experience of extraordinary depth and significance. When I had

read Shakespeare's Tragedies they had been for me a real
" katharsis ton pathematon ", a " purification of the passions ", as Aristotle had declared that tragedy should be.
But Shakespeare's heroes, Hamlet, Othello, Lear, Macbeth,
Antony, are all in their different ways the slaves of passion,
and the tragedy of this surrender to passion had seemed to
me to touch the deepest level of human experience. But
now Dante showed me that in the victory over passion there
is something greater than tragedy. Not by surrender to
passion nor by its suppression but by its transformation,
was the victory of life and of love to be won. This idea,
which underlies the whole of the *Divine Comedy* and is
revealed in the transformation of Dante's love of Beatrice
from the first passion of romantic love to its final transfiguration in the love of God in Paradise, was only very
imperfectly understood by me. In fact the *Paradiso* was
still so far beyond me that I hardly comprehended it at all.
But the *Purgatorio* stamped on my mind the fact that
moral virtue is the transformation of passion and not its
suppression, and so freed me for ever from the fear of
Puritanism.

But Dante had far more than this to give me. It was not
only his moral power but the vastness of his intellect which
astonished me. I had grown up to think of the Renaissance,
with Leonardo da Vinci and Michelangelo, Shakespeare
and Milton at its head, as the peak of European achievement. Now I could not fail to see that the mind of Dante
was immeasurably greater than that of Shakespeare or
Milton. At the same time I began to discover the painting
of Giotto and to see in it a power of imagination superior
to that of Botticelli or Michelangelo.

At this time Stanley Spencer, the painter, was living
within a short distance of my home and working on the
War Memorial chapel at Burghclere. I often went in to
see him at work and to talk to him at his home, and he
made me realise more than anyone else the greatness of
Giotto. I felt in his painting, with its religious insight into

the events of everyday life, something of the spirit of Giotto and he himself had something of the quality of a disciple of St Francis. He also taught me to appreciate the music of Bach. Thus in every way I was being driven back from my early romanticism and learning the beauty of an earlier and a greater art. But I could not help seeing also that behind Bach no less than behind Dante and Giotto there stood the massive power of a religion, which did not cramp the natural powers of man but on the contrary developed them to their highest point.

I now began to realise more of the inner meaning of that Gothic architecture which had so enthralled us at Lincoln and York. It was no longer simply the outward form of beauty, the triumph of craftsmanship and of the almost unconscious union of man with Nature which impressed me. I saw that behind all this there lay the power of a vast intelligence, not merely of an architectural genius but of a whole philosophy of life. I had up till this time never even heard the name of St Thomas Aquinas. At least I remember quite clearly when it first came into my consciousness as something of significance. It was when Lewis told me one day that a friend of his was reading Dante and had begun the study of St Thomas.

At this time the name of St Thomas was scarcely known in Oxford. His philosophy was not studied in any of the schools and he had no place in the curriculum. Even the *Metaphysics* of Aristotle was scarcely known to the ordinary student. In Greats the *Ethics* was studied but not the *Metaphysics* and as a result the whole of that system of philosophy which had been the foundation of the studies of medieval Oxford was practically unknown. We were still living by the light of that Renaissance humanism, to which Cicero was of more importance than St Thomas and Descartes of more value than St Augustine. It was some time before I began to read St Thomas for myself but already I saw his shadow cast on the poetry of Dante and I recognised in the ordered structure of Dante's thought and the comprehensiveness of his vision something of the grandeur and immensity of a great cathedral. I had still only a very imperfect conception of its real significance, but my mind was moving now towards the thirteenth century as the supreme period of European art and philosophy, and already I began to see the Renaissance as the initial stage in that decline of culture and spread of "civilisation" of which we were witnessing the last stages at the present day. It would not be true, however, to suggest that I was any nearer to Christianity, still less to any form of Catholicism; I was still thinking in terms of secular culture to which religion was merely a background.

This was the state of my mind as far as I can recall it, when I entered upon that great adventure in living which was to transform it so radically. Of course, in describing this development of my thought I have given it a logical consistency which it did not possess in reality. There were all the time innumerable movements and cross-currents of thought, which were often in conflict. I was like a man climbing a mountain, whose vision of the peak is often cut off, who loses himself in ravines and frequently takes false trails, and to whom the summit when it appears is veiled in mist. I was travelling on my own with very little guidance from others and exposed to all the dangers of inexperience. But now that I look back on it after twenty years I can see the pattern which was taking shape in my mind, just as the organs of an embryo can be seen in the process of their development by one who knows the structure of the finished organism. But in this case the actual process of thought has left such an impression on my mind that even after all these years I seem to live through it all again as I attempt to recall it. The effort of thought was so intense, the desire for a new life which I experienced was so fervent, the light which I received penetrated so deeply into my mind, that the marks of it remain in my soul like the grain in a tree, and I still feel it as part of a living process of thought which has never ceased.

But I should be giving a false impression of the direction in which my mind was moving if I were not to mention three other books of a totally different order which entered into the current of my thought at this time. These were the *Bhagavad Gita*, the Buddha's Way of Virtue (a version of the *Dhammapada*), and the *Sayings* of Lao Tzu (a version of the *Tao Te Ching*) in the Wisdom of the East series. I was introduced to these, as far as I can remember, by a friend of my mother, who was a theosophist. She was a remarkable woman who had been a suffragette and surprised us all as children by smoking cigarettes, a thing which was then unknown to us in a woman.

The influence of these books upon my life was later to be immense, and I still look on them as the three greatest books of spiritual wisdom outside the New Testament. I still possess the three little books with the markings in them which I made when I first read them. They were to act as a secret ferment in my soul and to colour my thought almost without my knowing it. After lying quiescent for many years, they again came back to me through a series of unexpected encounters and led on to a deeper study of the three great spiritual traditions for which they stand. But at this time I do not think that they did much more than give a wider non-Christian background to my thought. It was not that I found anything unchristian in them, but on the contrary that their doctrine seemed to me practically identical with that of Christianity as I understood it. From this time the Buddha and Lao Tzu took their place in my mind with Socrates, Spinoza and Marcus Aurelius, along with the Christ of the Sermon on the Mount, among the great spiritual leaders of mankind. But that was before I had begun seriously to read the Gospels for myself, an event which was to change my attitude completely. Yet the influence of this eastern thought was to remain as an undercurrent, as I have said, and the effort to bring it into relation with Christianity was to occupy me for many years, and indeed to continue to the present day.

CHAPTER FOUR

AN EXPERIMENT IN COMMON LIFE

It was in April 1930 that we set out upon our adventure. It was a time of crisis when to others beside ourselves our civilisation seemed to be in danger of collapse. The movement of parties to the extreme Left and the extreme Right was beginning, and many of our contemporaries at Oxford were turning to Communism. But for us politics offered no solution to the problem. The political parties, whether of the Left or the Right, were concerned only with the organisation of civilised life; but we were concerned with the very nature of our civilisation. Communism, as we saw it evolving in Russia, was working more and more for the mechanisation of life and therefore for that inhumanity which we believed must necessarily follow, though we were not then aware of the extent of the inhumanity to which it would lead. Our purpose was to escape from industrialism altogether, from the whole system of mechanisation which we felt to be the cause of the trouble. There was no doubt an element of escapism in our attitude, and there was certainly a radical inconsistency. For we were going to live on money which was derived from the system which we repudiated and we were dependent on it in a hundred ways which we could not escape. But though we were not unaware of the inconsistency in our position, we were determined to do what was in our power at least to escape from the evil influence. Whatever may be said for it in theory, in practice it was an experience which taught us a lesson in life which nothing else could have done. It not only forced us to face the fundamental problems of human life, of food and clothing and shelter, in their most elementary nature, but it also brought us into contact with a mode of life very close to that in which man has been compelled to live for the greater part of his history, and made a corresponding change in our own outlook. We passed at a single bound from the complexities of twentieth-century civilisation to a life which was primeval in its simplicity.

We began by buying a cottage in the small village of Eastington, about two miles from Northleach. It was a four-roomed cottage built of solid Cotswold stone with Cotswold tiling but without water, drainage or lighting of any sort. It was attached to another cottage of the same style, and we bought them both for £500. The second cottage was occupied by a young man, Jim Holtom, and his wife, who proved themselves among our best friends. Jim was driving a coal lorry at the time, but he had farming in his blood and spent all his spare time working on a small holding. His father was the shepherd of the farm on the hill above us and his brother was working on another farm. Jim soon agreed to work in with us and we bought some land and a couple of cows, and soon we were able to supply the whole village with milk. There were not more than twenty people altogether in the village, and all lived in small cottages like our own with Cotswold tiles, except for one, which had had the tiles stripped and sold to make money, and replaced by a hideous asbestos roof. We thus had always before our eyes an example of greed and industrialism bringing disharmony and ugliness into the ordered beauty of life.

The village had nothing particularly picturesque about it. It was a plain little village at the bottom of a valley with a small stream running through it, but it had the simple beauty of everything which is in harmony with nature. It will give some idea of the cost of living in these conditions if I say that the rent of most of these cottages was not more than three or four shillings a week, and yet each of them had a small garden and often a solid stone pig-sty as well. Jim Holtom's father, the shepherd, had brought up his family of five on a wage of twelve and six a week, and they had never lacked for any of the necessities of life. There were others living on the old age pension who, with the vegetables from their garden, a sow and perhaps some bees, could live in considerable comfort. They always welcomed us with a glass of home-made wine and would never take money for the vegetables which they gave us.

Our next-door neighbours were three brothers, one of whom was a devout Methodist, whose favourite books were the Bible, *Pilgrim's Progress* and Foxe's *Book of Martyrs*; but he was an epileptic, and it was a shock one day to find him, when I went to draw the water at the village tap, lying on his cabbage patch in a fit. Another brother was said to be an atheist. They lived in separate houses and it was said that they had never spoken to one another in twenty years. The inhabitants of the cottage with the asbestos roof were unmarried and had a bad reputation, which sometimes caused a disturbance in the village. But generally the life was very peaceful and we made friends of all.

There was no water laid on in the village and we all went to the village tap to draw water. Twenty years before, it was said, there had been no tap even and the villagers had gone to fetch their water from the spring. It was my job to fill the water-pots every morning, and often in the winter one would go out in the early morning before it was yet light and find the tap frozen; but we soon learned to light a straw fire underneath it on these occasions so as to thaw it. We had our own garden which Hugh used to work, and very soon we were able to grow most of our own vegetables. The only form of sanitation was an earth closet outside, and one of my first jobs was to clean this out and spread the contents on the garden for manure. We were thus faced from the start with the most primitive conditions of life, but it was exactly what we wanted. We were up by six o'clock every morning, and each of us learned to milk, so that our lives fell into the regular rhythm of the country. We had not to get up to see the dawn; it was there waiting for us when we went out to draw the water or to milk the cows, and morning and evening in winter we could watch the constellations moving round the sky.

Inside, the cottage was as bare and simple as we could make it. There were four rooms, a kitchen which we used also as a living-room, and another room, which we used as a study, downstairs; and two bedrooms upstairs, one of which we made into a dormitory and the other we kept as a spare room for our friends. The walls we had whitewashed and for ceiling there were the oak rafters stained with creosote. We picked up a kitchen table and some old wheel-back chairs second-hand, and apart from them we had no furniture. On the floor we had coconut-matting. Our beds were made of wood by the local carpenter and we had mattresses stuffed with straw from a neighbouring farm. We had no curtains or coverlets or cushions or anything to relieve the bare simplicity. All this was a matter of long discussion and often of argument between us, as we were not all alike in our tastes and it took time to work out the principles on which we wished to live. Our aim was to do without all products of the industrial revolution as far as it was humanly possible. At first we compromised in many things, but gradually we found that it was possible to go further than we had ever imagined. For instance, we had bought to begin with an oil lamp, but we later found a blacksmith who was willing to make us an iron candelabrum, and to our delight we discovered that it was possible to get tallow dips for candles, which had once been a local industry. We found, moreover, that the four candles gave a perfect light for reading; and we learned from this one of the great lessons of our life. Our purpose in using the tallow dips had been simply to do without the products of industrialism, but we found that the light of these candles, reflected on the bare white walls and against the dark oak rafters, created an atmosphere of indescribable beauty. Thus we were able to prove in our own lives that when the simple, natural means are used for any natural end, however humble, they will inevitably produce an effect of beauty.

Another problem which presented itself was that of crockery. There was an ironmonger's van which used to call each week in the village with oil which we bought at first for our oil lamp, and also with a stock of cheap modern ware. We thought at first that we should have to buy some of this, but when we asked the man he told us that there was a pottery at Winchcombe where we could get hand-made pots. The next day, therefore, I rode over to Winchcombe and was met at the pottery by an old man who, I discovered, was called Elijah Comfort. He told me that " the master " was inside and I went in, expecting to see another old man like himself. But I was met by a young man not much older than myself, who had been a contemporary at Oxford and had given up academic life in order to devote his life to the revival of the old English type of pottery known as slip-ware. This was Michael Cardew, whose work was already becoming well known and was afterwards exhibited at the Victoria and Albert Museum as some of the finest work of modern craftsmanship. But his desire was not to produce pots for exhibition but for the ordinary use of the house.

He soon became one of our closest friends and was ready to provide us with anything which we wanted and to make special pots for us if it was necessary. In this way we obtained all the crockery we needed, made out of the local clay and fashioned with the kind of instinctive beauty of the homely old English ware. Among other things he made us two superb pitchers for fetching the water from the village tap, which were large enough to last, when filled, for the whole day. Michael was a great admirer of Chinese pottery and culture, to such an extent that he had learned the language in order to be able to study the *Analects* of Confucius in Chinese. We found in him, therefore, a link

with the whole of that traditional culture which had existed
all over the world before the Industrial Revolution came
to destroy it. He was also a musician and had learned to
play the recorder, and sometimes when he was staying with
us he would entertain us with airs from Purcell or Palestrina.

We allowed ourselves no modern books or newspapers or
gramophone or wireless in the cottage, but for recreation
we learned some old English rounds which we used to sing
sitting together round the table. I remember one in particular by William Byrd made on the words of the psalm,
*"Non nobis Domine non nobis, sed nomini tuo da
gloriam"*. We sang it for the beauty of the melody and the
counterpoint, but the words nevertheless made a deep
impression on me and like so much else in our life were
prophetic of events which were to come. Our reading was
all in the literature of the sixteenth and seventeenth centuries or earlier, and even the books, as time went on, were
mostly early editions and folios. In this way we soaked ourselves in the traditions of the past and the modern world
became more and more remote. I used sometimes to go
and stand by the main road not two miles away and watch
the cars going by, and it seemed as far removed from our
life as ancient Rome or Babylon.

We used to travel at first on a bicycle but after a short
time we decided to give this up and buy a horse. We all
learned to ride simply by jumping on the horse's back and
riding bare-back round a field, and soon we were able to
ride for quite long distances. When we went home, as we
did from time to time, we would never go by train, as the
train stood for us above all things as the symbol of that
which had destroyed the peace and order of the countryside. At first I would go by bicycle, but when we had
given up the bicycle I decided to walk. It was, I think,
about seventy or eighty miles and I could just manage it by
staying at two places on the way. Every departure from
the village thus became an adventure, which was often

tiring but which gave one a deep sense of belonging to the country.

Our food was always very simple and we soon settled into a regular routine. For breakfast we had porridge which we cooked in an iron cauldron over-night and put in a hay-box until the morning. For dinner we had a vegetable stew which we prepared after breakfast and again put in the hay-box until dinner-time. With this we had cheese from a great round of "Double-Gloster" Cheese, which had once been the ordinary cheese of the locality. For supper we had eggs from four Khaki-Campbell ducks which we left to forage round the village all day and which laid four eggs without fail every morning. Our bread was baked for us by a baker at Bibury. We had wholemeal stone-ground flour from the old mill at Winchcombe, which was said to have been working since the Norman Conquest, and it was baked in an old brick oven heated by faggots.

In many ways like this, we found that the customs of former ages still survived in one or two places, though it is probable that they have now died out. I was told that twenty years before the old flour mills had been working in all the villages down the little river valleys, whereas now all the corn was sent to Cirencester to be ground by machinery. We were thus witnessing the death of a great cultural inheritance. For all around us in the Cotswold villages and towns we could see the remains of a local culture of authentic beauty. It had grown out of the country and developed century by century until it had formed a closely woven pattern of economic life, in which all the native skill of craftsmanship was able to reveal itself. It was a culture based on local custom and tradition, centred in small towns and villages, which were largely independent of the outside world, and which therefore had its own unique, distinctive character. The new world of the industrial towns was steadily destroying it, but at least we were able to learn some of the secrets of that way of life, which had sustained its existence for so many centuries.

We tried to live as far as possible without the use of anything which could not be obtained in the locality. Thus we had no tea or coffee or sugar or tobacco, but drank milk from the cows and used honey with which one of our neighbours supplied us for sweetening. We even tried to get our bread made from Cotswold wheat and our porridge from Cotswold oats. Of course, we were not pretending that it was possible to go back altogether to those earlier conditions of life, but we wanted to test for ourselves what life under such conditions was like. At least it taught us one lesson of permanent value. We found that the cost of living was lower than we could ever have imagined. We reckoned after some experiment that the three of us could live on an income of £100 a year altogether, allowing not only for food and clothing and all household expenses but also for books. On the other hand, if we went home for two or three days we would spend more in a day than would have kept us in the necessities of life for a week or a fortnight.

From this we learned that modern civilisation is not concerned primarily with providing the necessities of life any more than with producing those things which make for its beauty and dignity, but above all in extending the quantity of material conveniences. This served us as a criterion to distinguish between civilisation and culture. For while a civilisation is concerned with the continual extension of material luxury, often at the cost of the health and happiness of those who work for it, a culture like that of the Cotswolds, in which we were living, is based first of all on the necessities of human life, on the need for food and clothing and shelter. On this basis it builds up a network of human industry, in which the skill of men's hands is employed in co-operation with nature. The ploughing of the earth and the sowing and reaping of the corn; the tending of cattle and sheep for meat and leather and wool; the brewing of malt and baking of bread; the spinning and weaving for clothes; the quarrying of stone for building and the felling of timber for the carpenter's shop—all these were part of an age-long ritual in which it was understood that man's well-being was to be found. It was on this basis that the great cultures of antiquity had grown, of China and India no less than of Greece and Rome. Upon this basis the arts of architecture, sculpture, painting, poetry, music and dancing could develop, all in vital relationship with the common life of the town and village. A culture was an organic growth in which man and nature worked together in a profound harmony which satisfied the deepest instincts of the human heart.

This conception of the nature of a true culture was strengthened in my mind by the reading of Aristotle's *Ethics* and *Politics,* which were among the first books I now began to read. I read them in an old edition of the Greek without either dictionary or commentary, so as to be free from all modern influences. I must have missed a great deal of the meaning as a result, but the effort to wrestle with the thought of Aristotle in this way was an experience which I shall never forget. It was as though one could actually watch Greek thought taking shape under one's eyes. Aristotle had to form a philosophical language out of the material of ordinary human speech, and there is always as a result the sense of contact with human life and human needs, which one misses in Kant and in most modern thought. Here again I saw the same principle at work of a language growing organically out of the needs of human life, in contrast with the stereotyped language of a civilisation which is losing its roots in common life and becoming mechanised.

I used to read every morning without a fire in the room which we kept for study; in the winter my feet were often frozen at the end of the morning and I would have to take a walk to restore the circulation. This not only kept my brain clear but also quickened the sense of wrestling with facts and digging a meaning out of language. Thus, this reading of Aristotle was an experience of extraordinary depth. Before this I had always been a Platonist and the *Republic* had furnished my idea of the ideal state. But now I was converted to the realist method of Aristotle, who was not concerned in the construction of an ideal of pure reason, but set himself to discover how human beings had actually lived and governed themselves. He had in the Greek city states around him the most perfect material for the study of human nature and human politics, because life was still near to its primitive origins but was being lived and organised by the most intelligent people on earth.

The result of this is that the *Ethics* and the *Politics* of Aristotle form the most penetrating study of human nature and the organisation of human life which has ever been made. It was the *Politics* which affected me most deeply. For the first time I began to see the place of kingship in human life. I saw that the institution of kingship with its roots going back to the primitive patriarchal order of life was the means by which the continuity of tradition is preserved. A culture can only grow organically if this continuity is preserved not only in economic but also in political life. I was reading Clarendon's history of the Great Rebellion at the same time and it formed a perfect historical commentary on Aristotle. I saw how in seventeenth-century England the same forces had been at work as in fourth-century Greece, and the same process had followed. There was the same conflict in England as in Greece between king and nobles and people; and in both alike, kingship and aristocracy had given way first to oligarchy then to plutocracy and finally to democracy, which as Aristotle saw always tended to lead to tyranny. The dictator had already risen in Europe to prove the correctness of Aristotle's diagnosis, and the reign of plutocracy was only too evident.

I could see more clearly now that the Industrial Revolution was not merely the cause of the mechanisation of life but also of the rise to power of the merchant and tradesman. In Greek society as in all the great cultures of the ancient world, the merchant had always been regarded with some contempt as one of the lowest types of men in the state. The constant aim of Greek culture, as of the Chinese and the Indian, had been to keep the power in the hands of the " wise man ", the philosopher, the Brahmin or the Mandarin, and after him with the nobleman or aristocrat, and by this means the character of their culture had been preserved. In Greece as in Rome and in modern England, the rise of a plutocracy had transferred the power to the merchant, and the decline of culture into material civilisation had followed.

I began to regard the seventeenth century now as the Golden Age in English history. It was a time of violent conflict when all the forces which were to shape modern history were coming into being, but it was also a time when the traditional order of life was still preserved. The conflict in religion between the Established Church and Non-Conformity, in politics between the King and Parliament, in economic life between the new merchant class and the old aristocracy, in thought between the new science and philosophy and the ancient tradition, was the fire in which all these different elements had to be welded into English life. But the battle was fought out within the framework of the ancient tradition and the continuity of tradition was preserved. As a result, the culture of the seventeenth century was of supreme beauty. It had the rich vitality of an ancient culture receiving new life from new ways of life and thought. This could be seen in the prose of Clarendon as in that of Donne and Jeremy Taylor, of Milton and Sir Thomas Browne. There was a grandeur and a dignity in men's lives as well as in their thoughts, and yet it was combined with the homely simplicity which one found in Walton's Lives of Hooker and George Herbert. This inevitably drew my attention to the religion of these men, which as I could see more and more clearly, underlay the whole of their culture. It was reflected in the Cotswold towns and villages among which we were living, where the great perpendicular churches, built in the later Middle Ages with the money made in the wool trade, still stood as the visible symbol of that religion around which so much conflict had raged and still towered over the cottages and market squares, the farmsteads and manor-houses of the countryside. Thus, beneath the economic and political structure I was led to study the religion which had sustained it for so many centuries and which had already begun to make a strong appeal to me.

It was in these circumstances that I began to read the Bible. We had each of us obtained an old Black Letter edition of the Authorised Version of the Bible. We began to read them first of all for their literary interest, as part of that great tradition of seventeenth-century prose to which we were all alike attached. It soon became part of our regular routine to sit down every day before breakfast round the table with our Bibles spread out before us, while the porridge was cooking on the fire and the candles in winter shed their mellow light on the crockery. I used to read a chapter of the Old Testament and a chapter of the New Testament in this way every day, and in the course of the next year or two I must have read the Bible through two or three times. It now became part of the habitual background of my life; but it very soon ceased to be of merely literary interest.

The life which we were living in this lonely village among the hills, spending much of our time under the open sky and watching the changes of the season and the routine of life on the farms around, gave to the stories of the Bible an intimate reality. The stories of Abraham and Isaac and Jacob, or Moses and David, pasturing their flocks, had a living meaning for us when we went out at lambing time and saw the shepherd tending the young lambs, and watched how, when a ewe had lost her lamb, he would take another lamb and cover it with the dead lamb's coat, so that the ewe might take it for her own : or again how he would take a weak or sick lamb home and feed it by bottle, so that it became part of the household. The background of the Old Testament was the background of our own lives, and its people and their story were not of a remote past but of a living present.

Even as literature it seemed to me to be greater than anything I had ever read. The stories had all the poetic quality of the *Iliad* and the *Odyssey* and at the same time the vivid historical sense of Herodotus or Thucydides. When I compared this Hebrew literature as a whole with Greek literature as I had known it, I could not but think that it was greatly superior. I felt this particularly in regard to the book of Job. Here was a poem, a poetic drama, a tragedy which could be compared with the work of Aeschylus or Sophocles or Shakespeare. Its descriptions of nature were, I felt, of a power which had never been surpassed, and its portrayal of suffering seemed to go deeper than King Lear. The drama had not the economy and the concentrated force of the Oedipus Tyrannus or the variety and range of Lear, but it went deeper into the mystery of suffering. It was no longer the working out of an inevitable law or a conflict of passion which must always issue in tragedy. Like everything in nature, it was referred to a cause beyond this human scene, in which the whole meaning of human life and suffering was to be found. The significance of Job was not to be found in the happy ending which terminated the tragedy, but in the last words of Job : " I had heard of thee by the hearing of the ear; but now mine eye seeth thee, wherefore I abhor myself and repent in dust and ashes." Job had experienced the reality of the divine presence not only in its power to wound but in its utter transcendence, and in the face of this he himself and all his sufferings seemed to count as nothing. Here I seemed to be touching the very heart of the revelation of the Old Testament. It was not a rational explanation of the nature of God in the manner of Spinoza; it was the record of an experience, of a meeting with God, the supreme reality, which had changed men's lives. When God spoke to Abraham, when Moses met him in the Burning Bush, when Samuel heard him calling, these were events of vital significance which determined the lives of men and peoples. They were experiences of the soul which gave a new meaning to existence; that was why they had such a poetic character.

I had always understood it to be the function of the poet to see beneath the surface of nature and of human life and to reveal its inner meaning. The beauty to be found in the poem was an index of the degree of truth and insight to which the poet had attained. Hardy and Conrad, Shelley and Keats, Shakespeare and Sophocles, had led me so far; but now I seemed to have been taken a step further. In the Old Testament the reality behind nature and behind the conflicts of human life had been encountered at a level of significance beyond anything that I had known before. These encounters were an experience of the soul in its inmost depths, an experience not of the mind alone but of the mind and will, the imagination and the senses. They issued therefore not in scientific formulæ or in philosophical concepts, but in poetry, in dramatic representation, in a living history. It was history because it was the living encounter of men with reality, which changed their lives and shaped the course of affairs; but it was also poetry because it was an experience of the soul penetrating beneath the surface of life and encountering the hidden power which directs and controls it. And this power revealed itself not merely as the Beauty, which underlies all the forms of nature; not merely as the Truth which philosophy discerns beneath the appearances of things; but as a moral power, a power of Good, which made inexorable demands on men and could only be conceived as a living person. Whatever judgment one might eventually pass on this conception, its poetic power could not be denied. It had the reality of authentic experience and had to be reckoned with in any attempt to face the problem of life.

The message of the Hebrew prophets came to me with the force of a revelation : I saw in it a judgment on our own civilisation more profound than I had ever envisaged. Our civilisation was not merely an offence against beauty and truth, against that rational order of life upon which human culture is based. It was an offence against the moral order of the universe. I saw in the great civilisations of Babylonia and Egypt, of the Greek and the Roman Empires, the exact counterpart of our own civilisation. There was to be seen in each of them the same degeneration from a primitive culture to a gross material civilisation, the same extension of material convenience at the expense of creative energy, the same tendency to dull uniformity. But now I saw that deeper than this there was the same breakdown of morality, the exploitation of the poor by the rich and their systematic enslavement, and all this was traced by the prophets to their rejection of God, to that moral order which man encounters when he lives according to his conscience and which gradually becomes obliterated in his eyes by his subjection to the material world. Nor was this voice of the prophets the kind of moralising to which I had objected in the past. It was not an abstract moral system imposed on life : it was a moral order discerned with poetic insight at the very heart of life. It was akin to the intuition of the great poet or the great novelist, like Tolstoy or Dostoevsky, who sees into the heart of man and discovers the hidden motives of his actions. But here it was not merely individual men who were concerned. The vision of the prophet looked into the hearts of nations; he discovered the inner meaning of history, the principles which govern the destiny of nations. The source of evil was to be found in the human mind rising up against God and seeking to build up its civilisation without reference to God, the supreme arbiter of destiny, whose will was the ultimate source of all human happiness. The error of modern civilisation could now be seen to lie not merely in the divorce of the scientific mind from the imagination and the sources of creative life; but in its revolt against the moral order of the universe, in its deliberate rejection of the authority of God. It was but one more instance in the long tale of man's pride and rebellion against God.

The Greeks, and in particular Aeschylus, had understood the danger of this pride, which they called "hubris", and they had known that it is inevitably visited with disaster; but they had not been able to discover its source in the original disobedience of man to that law which governs the universe and is inscribed in his own inmost being. The Hebrew prophet had learned that behind the whole movement of history, as behind every human life, there is to be found not merely an abstract moral law, but a personal will, which man encounters when he enters into the depths of his being and upon which the well-being of men and of nations depends.

It would be difficult to say how long it was before this message penetrated into my mind. In a sense, no doubt, it was the work of years, but already, I think, it had taken root. When I went on to read the Hebrew Wisdom literature, I was no less deeply affected. Here was a "wisdom" which challenged comparison with the wisdom of Greek philosophy, and again I could not but feel that it went deeper. "The fear of the Lord is the beginning of wisdom" struck a new note in my ear, and though its real meaning was still far from me, I had already begun to realise that the problem with which I was concerned was not merely a problem of art and philosophy but a problem of religion. Once again, though, it was the poetic quality of the Proverbs and Ecclesiastes which appealed to me first, the personification of wisdom crying aloud in the streets, and the haunting music of the conclusion of Ecclesiastes: "Remember also thy Creator in the days of thy youth or ever the evil days come and the years draw nigh when thou shalt say, I have no pleasure in them."

But even more I was fascinated by the books of the Apocrypha, that is, those books which belonged to the later Greek canon of the Bible and were mostly written in Greek. Here I found something of the Greek philosophical spirit united with the religious spirit of the Hebrew. In particular, I was attracted to the Wisdom of Solomon (a book which does not go back to Solomon but to the late Alexandrian era), where I felt again the enthusiasm for wisdom which had inspired Spinoza. Most precious of all was the discovery in it of a sense of the immanence of God in the universe. Here was a link with Spinoza himself, showing that the God whom I had conceived as the source of the rational order of the universe was one with the God of Hebrew prophecy.

I shall never forget the emotion with which I read the words about wisdom : " For there is in her a spirit quick of understanding, holy, alone in kind, manifold, subtil, freely moving, clear in utterance, unpolluted, distinct, unharmed, loving what is good, keen, unhindered, beneficent, loving towards man, steadfast, sure, free from care, all-powerful, all-surveying, and penetrating through all spirits that are quick of understanding, pure, most subtil : for wisdom is more mobile than any emotion; yea, she pervadeth and penetrateth all things by reason of her pureness. For she is a breath of the power of God and a clear effluence of the glory of the Almighty; therefore can nothing defiled find entrance into her. For she is an effulgence from everlasting light, and an unspotted mirror of the working of God and an image of his goodness. And she being one hath power to do all things; and remaining in herself, reneweth all things : and from generation to generation passing into holy souls she maketh them friends of God and prophets."

Here it seemed was the wisdom of Spinoza and of Marcus Aurelius, that law which they had perceived to underlie the universe, ordering all the forces of nature and reflected in the reason and the moral life of man, now related to its source in the transcendent power of God. Here in this final

phase of Hebrew revelation was to be seen the reconcilia-
tion of religion and philosophy which I had glimpsed in
Dante and St Augustine, but which I now perceived had its
roots in the Old Testament itself. By this time I had
already advanced into the New Testament and begun to
make new discoveries.

CHAPTER FIVE

THE BEGINNING OF FAITH

I began the New Testament with St Mark's Gospel, because I thought that this was the most primitive and that there if anywhere was to be found the authentic portrait of Christ. I expected to find there the figure of the human Christ, free from all the accretions of later legend, which had been familiar to me from my boyhood, but as soon as I began to read for myself I found that it was very different from what I had been led to suppose. The human figure was there certainly as real and living as the figure of Socrates in the Apology and the early dialogues of Plato. There was no mistaking its actuality; it had all the roughness and unexpectedness which one finds in a character from life as opposed to the smoothness and conventionality of legend and the ideal portrait. But with this element of realism and of living humanity there was another element, that of the supernatural, which was no less evident than the first, nor was this something which could be easily detached, leaving the human figure unimpaired. The two elements were woven together into the substance of the Gospel, so that they could not be separated without doing violence to it. The miracles were described with the same graphic realism as the other events, and clearly belonged to the same structure. In the same way the human teaching which I had always loved was implicated, I found, with supernatural claims of an astonishing kind, which had the same quality of authentic utterance. It was this character of authenticity which impressed me above everything. I approached the Gospels in the same frame of mind as I had approached the Apology of Socrates, the Meditations of Marcus Aurelius or the Confessions of St Augustine, and I judged them by

83

the same standard. I could no more doubt the quality of the character and personality revealed in them than I could doubt that of Socrates or Marcus Aurelius. It was clearly the authentic voice of truth, and if there were elements in the teaching which I could not properly understand, I was prepared to accept them as I accepted them in Plato or St Augustine. I could wait until further light was given.

This authentic speech was intimately related to the facts which were recorded, so that the one could not be separated from the other. The climax of the whole story, for instance, turned on the answer of Christ to the question of the High Priest: " Art thou the Christ, the Son of the Blessed?" : when he replied unequivocally: "I am." It was clearly impossible to dismiss this as an accretion; it was the keystone in the structure of the whole. So when I came to consider the question of the miracles, especially the Resurrection, I had to ask myself: "Could they be abstracted from the whole without destroying the structure?" and it was clear that they could not. The evidence for the Resurrection in St Mark was of the same factual character as the rest, and was all the more striking for its extreme brevity. The problem of reconciling the three accounts of the Resurrection, which had disturbed me so long ago, now appeared in quite a new light.

When I turned to St Matthew and St Luke, I found in them the same kind of actuality as in St Mark, though there was not quite the same realism. Yet in certain ways it appeared that St Matthew was nearer to the original speech of Christ, particularly in the Sermon on the Mount. Here if anywhere was the authentic voice of the teacher, and yet once again could it be detached from the whole? The structure of St Matthew was different; there was a considerable difference in tone: but there was the same inner coherence, the same sense of an organic whole. Again St Luke was different from St Matthew; he was a Greek writing for Greeks, while St Matthew was a Jew writing for

Jews; he was perhaps further removed from the source : but there were elements in his Gospel like the parables of the Good Samaritan and the Prodigal Son, which were clearly as authentic as anything in St Matthew or St Mark.

So when I came to compare the different accounts of the Resurrection I was not troubled by the apparent discrepancies. Here were three distinct accounts of the same event, all with the same quality of actuality, depending on the evidence of eye-witnesses, differing in detail and in point of view, and yet all clearly bearing witness to the same fact. There was no harmonisation, or smoothing out of the differences; the stories were left to speak for themselves by their candour and originality. Always I came back to this overwhelming impression of truthfulness, that quality of truth which I sought in all literature, and which I had learned to recognise by the beauty, the rightness, of its expression. Judged simply as literature, the essential truth of the Gospels could not be doubted, but this truth was a truth not merely of idea but of fact, of history; the two were so interwoven that they could not be separated. I could not, of course, pass a final judgment on them at this stage, and it was many years before my mind became clear on the subject; but the first impression was that there was a solid objective truth in the Gospels which had to be faced. When I read the accounts of the Virgin Birth in St Matthew and St Luke, my impression was the same. They both had an extremely primitive character; one had only to compare them with the stories of the Golden Legend to see the difference between pious fancy and recorded fact. Perhaps the conditions of life in which I was living helped me to see this also. It was difficult to imagine the Annunciation taking place in London or Birmingham any more than in any of the great cities of the Roman Empire. It had taken place in a remote village among the hills of Galilee, and I found no difficulty in believing that it might have taken place in one of our Cotswold villages. Here in the country men's minds were open to the wonder of the natural and the supernatural world, which the civilisation of the towns hid from them.

What, after all, was my objection to the supernatural? Was it not one of those prejudices of the scientific mind, which I believed to be the cause of the impoverishment and the degradation of human life? The scientific mind could never get beyond the phenomena of the external world, and by mistaking its mathematical abstractions for the ultimate reality was depriving human life of all meaning. I had learned that behind the phenomena of nature there is a power which is not only the source of their existence but also the cause of all their acts; and I had come to believe that this power was not only a rational power but also a moral power, which revealed itself as a personal will. Was it not possible that this will could not only reveal itself to the mind of the prophet but could also act through him on the phenomenal world? What difficulty was there in believing that that wisdom, which I had learned from the Wisdom of Solomon penetrates all things by reason of its pureness, could not only work through the ordinary laws of nature, but could also transcend them? I do not think that my mind was at all clear about this for some time, but I realised certainly that I had been a victim of prejudice about the supernatural, and that this must now be discarded along with all the other prejudices of the modern mind.

When I turned to St John's Gospel I was confronted with a graver problem. It was clear that it differed completely not only in its point of view, but still more in its whole style and character. And yet I could not but be impressed again with its factual nature. It was as close to the actuality of history in certain respects as St Mark, and once more the discourses however different their tone and bearing, were no less closely interwoven with the facts. I did not attempt to reconcile their differences, but again I judged the impression of St John's Gospel as a whole. It was clear that this was one of the most significant works of human genius. Whatever its precise import might be, it was the record of an experience of unfathomable depth. Both the person and the doctrine portrayed were of a beauty beyond all human imagination; there was nothing in Plato which could be compared with them. I realised that to reject this would be to reject the greatest thing in all human experience; on the other hand, to accept it would be to change one's whole point of view. It would be to pass from reason and philosophy to faith.

Already I had begun to see that to do this would be to place oneself with St Augustine and with Dante : it would be to enter into that tradition, which on other grounds I had learned to love and respect. Might it not be that within this tradition one would discover the meaning of the whole? Modern criticism had been engaged in tearing the Gospels to pieces to discover the truth behind them, but might it not be that their true meaning could only be seen as a living whole, and that Christian tradition could give one this sense of the whole, by which all the apparently conflicting elements were integrated? In judging a work of art, it was by one's sense of the whole, of an integral organic structure, that one was able to see the significance of the parts. Might there not be a sense of the whole, a spiritual perception, by which the inner meaning of the Gospel would be revealed?

But before I had to answer this question, I had begun to read St Paul, and here a new experience awaited me. I began with the Epistle to the Romans and I was immediately struck by St Paul's condemnation of the pagan world in the first chapter. I could not but see in it a condemnation of our own civilisation. The very vices which St Paul picked out were those of which I had been most conscious at Oxford. What impressed me was not the fact of vice, but the reason which St Paul gave for it. It was because " knowing God, they glorified Him not as God, neither gave thanks, but became vain in their reasonings and their senseless heart was darkened ". Was not this the spectacle which the modern world presented, the rejection of the reality of God through the "vain reasonings" of a false science, leading first to "senselessness" and then to immorality?

St Paul went further than this. He faced the problem of morality as I had never seen it done before. Our problem at Oxford had been that of immorality on the one side and an inhuman loveless morality on the other, and we had tried to find in Blake's conception of love and imagination a way between the two. But now I found St Paul facing the same problem far more profoundly. He saw the immorality of the pagan world on the one hand, but he saw no less clearly the insufficiency of the "Law" on the other. The "Law" stood in St Paul's mind, of course, for the Mosaic Law primarily, but the Mosaic Law, framed in the Ten Commandments, was typical of the law of Morality, of Conscience, as a whole. It was the insufficiency of conscience and morality which St Paul was proclaiming. In his eyes the moral and strictly religious Pharisee was no better than the immoral pagan; he might indeed be worse, just as Christ had found the Pharisee worse than the publican and the sinner.

This was surely a revelation of the modern dilemma. We had reacted against the conventional morality of the Victorian Age only to fall into irreligion and immorality. But St Paul showed that there was another way, and it was very near to the way of love and imagination which we had tried to find. St Paul's love was something more than human love; it was a gift of God, a means of transcending the limitations of human love, such as we had never conceived. And what was St Paul's substitute for imagination? It was faith; but was not faith the very thing which we had been blindly seeking with our theory of the imagination? For us the imagination had been the power to see beyond the phenomenon, to grasp that reality which underlies the appearances of this world. I knew now that this reality was not merely an idea (in the Platonic sense), but a will. Would not faith be the reaching out of the human will towards that universal will, the discernment of its presence in the person of Christ?

By now I was prepared to face St Paul's doctrine of Original Sin. I no longer had any illusions about the nature of man. I could see that not only our own civilisation but all the civilisations of the past revealed the same tendency towards corruption. St Paul now showed me that this was something in the very nature of man; that his nature was corrupted and that the effects of this corruption were inevitable. The history of our own civilisation, its rejection of God, its development of a false science, its materialism, its immorality, was simply the history of all human civilisation. The "world" as such was evil; it was in a state of "sin". Against this St Paul set a new hope; there was a possibility of another kind of life than that of the world. It was a passage in the first epistle to the Corinthians which first gave me light on this. I remember writing a long letter to Lewis at this time on the text, "As in Adam all die, even so in Christ shall all be made alive". I don't know exactly what I said, but I think I saw clearly now that as we all inherit a nature which has the tendency to evil in it, so we may all receive a new nature in Christ. By this I understood that there is an organic unity in mankind; we all inherit the same nature and we all receive the promise of a new nature in Christ. It was then that for the first time the real meaning of the Church dawned on my mind. Until this time I do not think that it had ever been more than a social institution in my eyes. Now I realised that the Church was nothing less than this new humanity. It was a social order indeed, but it was an order that transcended this world, that is to say, all human civilisation. It was a social organism of which Christ was the "head" and all men were potentially its members.

Now when I put all this together in my mind, my way became clear. I saw now that underlying that seventeenth-

century culture which I so much admired lay the solid
strength of the Christian tradition. It was in rejecting this
that our civilisation had gradually fallen from its original
greatness to its present state of decay. After reading
Clarendon's history of the rebellion, I went on to read
Hooker's *Laws of the Ecclesiastical Polity,* and there I
found just that basis in religion for which I was looking.
Once again it was a masterpiece of English prose, which
appealed to me for its grandeur and beauty, but also for
its solid doctrine. I found there the doctrine of the mystical Body of Christ expounded with wonderful power, and
I thought that in the Church of England, as Hooker conceived it, I could find the living reality of the Church. Here
I thought was the link between St Paul and St Augustine
and Dante; here in the Church of England could be found
the living contact with the past which I wanted; here was
that tradition to be found which would give meaning to the
whole and bring me into touch with the Church of the
Gospels. I went along, therefore, to the church at Northleach, a grand perpendicular church of the fifteenth century in which the traditions of the past seemed to be embodied, and there I met a young priest who had been
recently ordained and was a sincere Anglo-Catholic. He
confirmed me in my view and from that time I began once
again to go to Communion in the Church of England.

In the meantime we had already begun to practise our
own religion. It was Hugh who first suggested that we
should begin to pray as well as to read the Bible, but the
step was almost inevitable. I had not prayed since I had
been at school, but the change which had now taken place
in my mind made it seem natural to do so, and the Book of
Common Prayer offered a perfect method of prayer. The
Psalms and the Canticles of the Gospel in Coverdale's version came to me as poetry in a way that made the transition
to prayer almost imperceptible. I had gone to the poetry of
Wordsworth, Shelley and Keats in my early days at school
in order to find my experience of the mystery and beauty of

nature renewed and enlarged; for poetry is the means by which the feelings and the imagination are educated and their powers developed. Then my vision of human life and especially of its underlying tragedy had been extended by Shakespeare and Sophocles and by the great novelists. Now my horizon was being enlarged and the mystery of God's dealings with humanity and with the individual soul became apparent to me through my reading of the Bible. But it was the same path of imaginative experience which I had been following all the time; and now I found that the words of the Psalms came to me like pure poetry awaking the sense of God's power over nature and His providence over the human soul, and I prayed the Psalms almost without realising it.

Nevertheless a definite break was made in our lives when we began to pray on our knees. We used to kneel on the bare stone floor, not in the kitchen but out in the cold at the back of the house, and the words seemed to pierce the soul. Our life had already become extremely ascetic in many ways, not so much from any deliberate choice, but simply as the result of the way of life which we had adopted. Now we began to think of practising some deliberate austerity. Again, it was Hugh who suggested that we should fast on Fridays. This we did by taking nothing but some dry bread and cold milk throughout the day. There is no doubt that this was very unwise. We were none of us really prepared for such a penance and it imposed a great strain upon us. I myself began to read also the Imitation of Christ, which we had in a beautiful edition of the Early English Text Society. It was typical of our attitude that we read it first as an example of medieval prose; but its message made itself felt none the less, and I began to feel a desire for some kind of mortification; but it was very feeble and I could not stand up to any real privation.

By this time, however, our life had begun to develop along lines which none of us had envisaged, and a division began to take place among us. Hugh, though naturally religious, was of a very sociable character, and the austerity of the life told on him more than on any of us. He was the first to break away and to declare after his return from home at Christmas that he intended to get married. He later returned to Oxford to take his degree and then took a job as a schoolmaster. But he afterwards joined his wife's father on his farm and has remained a farmer ever since, bringing up his family on his own farm.

While we were together at Eastington two little children came to stay with us, a girl and a boy. The girl afterwards became Martyn's wife, and he also went to live on a farm taking Jim Holtom and his family with him. Thus in different ways our adventure at Eastington was the decisive event in all our lives. It only lasted for less than a year, but it taught us the lessons of a life-time. Our attitude to life had been radically changed, and we each of us drew from it the experience which was to shape our lives for the future, however far apart they might be.

I myself returned home and took a job for a short time tutoring a small boy. This only took up an hour or two of my time each day and so I was able to continue my reading as before. I think that I then first began to read the *Summa Theologica* of St Thomas Aquinas. This had been at the back of my mind ever since I had read Dante, and it came to me as a wonderful new adventure in thought. I concentrated especially on the first twenty-six questions on the nature and attributes of God. This brought back memories of Spinoza. There was the same rigorously logical method and the same fascination of a perfectly lucid mind. I was now finding the complete philosophical justification for Christianity. It was not so much any particular element in St Thomas's doctrine which impressed me as the sense of a comprehensive mind which had faced all the most difficult problems in regard to the existence and the nature of God and could present a reasoned judgment on them. I was particularly struck by the fact that the anthropomorphism of the Old Testament presented no difficulty to the mind of

St Thomas. The wrath of God, for instance, which presented such a difficulty to a logical mind, was simply explained as a metaphor.

My first impression, as I have said, was rather of the
greatness of the whole. It was like entering a great Gothic
cathedral. One might not understand all the principles of
its construction but one could not doubt that it was a
masterpiece of the human genius. Height upon height
opened up, displaying the endless variety of the most subtle
intelligence as all the resources of Greek philosophy were
brought to bear on the problems presented by Hebrew
revelation. I knew now what I had surmised before, that
the art of Dante and Giotto and the great cathedrals was
based on a solid structure of philosophy and theology, to
which the modern world could show no parallel. The range
of the human intellect had reached its highest peak in the
thirteenth century and what we had mistaken for the peak
in the sixteenth century was really the first level of a continuous descent.

At the same time, I happened to find a set of the works of
St Augustine and of St John Chrysostom in a second-hand
bookshop in Oxford, which I bought for a pound at a
shilling a volume, and I began to read some of them. I was
amazed to think that we had spent so much time at Oxford
reading all through Cicero and Demosthenes, while these
great masters of Greek and Latin prose were completely
ignored. I realised then how much our education had been
determined by the taste of Renaissance humanism, which
had turned its back on the great achievement of the
Christian centuries and gone for its inspiration to pagan
sources.

During this time I continued to go to Communion regularly in the Church of England, and the beauty of the
Communion service was a constant delight to me. I also
continued to read the Anglican divines of the seventeenth
century, in whom I found more and more the perfection of
that piety, which appealed to me, based on the Bible and

the Fathers and expressed in the most magnificent prose. I read some of T. S. Eliot's essays on this period also, which inspired me to buy a folio volume containing ninety sermons by Bishop Andrewes, the great Elizabethan divine, and I believe that I read it all through from beginning to end. I began to be attracted also to T. S. Eliot's political idea of a new Toryism based on the ideals of the seventeenth century. It happened that our Member for Parliament at that time was Lord Lymington, a young Tory peer, who had devoted himself to the development of farming on his own estates and who shared this ideal of a democracy based on agriculture and renewing the hierarchical traditions of the past. I wanted to see above all a renewal of agriculture and craftsmanship, such as had existed in the past, and this I thought might be brought about by a new Toryism which should separate itself from capitalism and re-establish the old order of independent ownership, as far as it was possible within a modern democracy.

But my dream of a return to the past was to be rudely interrupted. Again it was a book which suddenly gave my thoughts a new direction. I began to read Bede's *Ecclesiastical History of England*. My knowledge of England in the Middle Ages must have been very vague. At school our study of history had begun with the Tudors, and what I knew of the Middle Ages came from Scott's novels. At Oxford I had read Anglo-Saxon literature and had learned to admire the work of Alfred the Great. I had also a great love not only for Chaucer but also for William Langland, whose *Piers Plowman* was for me the authentic voice of that rural England which I loved, where the ploughman was seen to be a figure of Christ and the life of the common man was felt to be something sacred because Christ had entered into it and shared it with him. But my conception of medieval England never seems to have included the Church except as a vague background. I had never asked myself what the medieval Church was and what was its relation to life in England and Europe. I suppose that in a general way I had accepted the common opinion of a corrupt ecclesiastical system which had been cleaned up by the Reformation. Now when I read the pages of Bede's *History of the Church of England* from the earliest times, my whole perspective was changed.

It is a book of great charm, written by one who was unique in his time as a scholar and a historian; it recreates the life of the Church in the seventh century, to which Bede belonged, in the most exact detail. This short period in English history stands out from the almost universal darkness of this period like a scene from an illuminated manuscript, with all the accuracy of precise personal knowledge. The discovery that the Church of England had been founded by a Roman Pope and that the first Archbishops of Canterbury and York had been sent from Rome came as a new light to me. It was as though there had been a blank space in my map on history; which was now filled in, so that the whole was seen in a new perspective. Instead of looking back from the Renaissance to the Middle Ages, I now began to see the Middle Ages emerging from the Roman Empire, and the history of England took its place in the history of Europe. I saw that just as England had been part of the Roman Empire, so the Church of England had been part of the Roman Church. Before, it had always stood somehow outside the world of Dante and St Thomas; now I could see that it was an integral part of that same world; that it belonged to medieval Christendom.

It may seem strange but it had never occurred to me before that our old English village churches had once known the rite of the Latin Mass. I had always associated them with the Book of Common Prayer and their original status had gone unquestioned. Indeed I do not think that the Church of Rome had ever impinged consciously on my life, but now that it had appeared on the horizon, I realised that it was something which would have to be faced, and I went on to read Newman's *Apologia Pro Vita Sua*. This inevitably struck me with tremendous force. For

Newman had followed the same path as I had been following, basing himself on the Bible and the Fathers and the Anglican divines of the seventeenth century. And now I found that Newman with his vastly greater learning had found that position untenable. I was so seriously disturbed by this that I decided that I would have to visit a Roman Catholic church and at least find out something about it.

It is difficult to describe the fear with which the Roman Church filled me. It was, no doubt, partly the fear of the unknown. The Roman Church had always been for us as a family, as my father once expressed it, " outside the pale ". It was something strange and remote and essentially foreign to English life. I had known of one Catholic family in the village where we had lived as children but I had never spoken to any member of it. At school there had been a little group which used to go off to mass on Sunday mornings, but they were regarded as people with strange customs, like Jews, and I never spoke to one. At Oxford a Catholic undergraduate was once pointed out to me (we were to meet years later when we were both Benedictine monks), but it was only a matter of curiosity to me. I had never as far as I know spoken to anyone. And deeper than this fear of the unknown there was an inherited family prejudice against anything to do with Catholicism. I remember my mother once said that nothing would give her greater pain than that anyone she loved should become a Roman Catholic. Little did I know that I whom she loved so much was to be the cause of this pain to her. Behind this family feeling there was also a deeper feeling still, the prejudice which every Englishman inherits from the racial memory. The breach with Rome is a psychic event in all our lives, something which lies deep buried in the unconscious, but is ready to erupt into consciousness whenever circumstances force us to encounter it. It was this monster from the unconscious depths of my soul which I had now to face.

I went down to the Catholic church in Newbury one

Sunday morning to attend the mass. The priest noticed me when I entered, perhaps because I was feeling nervous and looked frightened, and took me up to the front of the church, which somewhat embarrassed me. The service was almost completely unintelligible to me. It was all as strange and in some way as terrifying as one might imagine a service in a Hindu temple. The ringing of bells and the smoke of incense and the muttering of unintelligible words created an atmosphere of mystery which was both attractive and repulsive. It attracted by its mystery, it repelled by its strangeness and uncouthness. The sermon was the only thing which I understood and that was in an idiom and a mode of thought so strange that I felt simply bewildered. I remember also that the requests for prayers for the dead and the reference to the state of Purgatory rather disturbed me. Altogether it was an experience which rather increased my fear. To study Catholicism in Dante and St Thomas was one thing, but to face it in its modern dress was very different; just as a student of the Vedanta would be shocked to face the religion of a Hindu temple.

However, I summoned up courage to speak to the priest afterwards and he took me into the presbytery and spoke to me about the See of Peter and the infallibility of the Pope. My mind was not prepared for this, and he made a fatal mistake by speaking contemptuously of Hooker and his doctrine of the Mystical Body of Christ. This doctrine was the very heart of what religion I possessed and Hooker was dear to me not only as a great and learned man but also as a lovable and holy person. I went away, therefore, not only with my fears increased but also with a sense of injury and a grave doubt as to the wisdom of my instructor.

I had for some time been considering the possibility of taking orders in the Church of England, and not long after this I rode over to Oxford to see the Principal of Cuddesdon College. On the way I debated with myself on the doctrine of the Roman Church and all my previous habits of thought began to reassert themselves. I thought of the

Authorised Version of the Bible and the Book of Common Prayer, of Hooker and Andrewes and Jeremy Taylor, of the poets, George Herbert and Henry Vaughan and Thomas Traherne; of all the inheritance of seventeenth-century England, the cathedrals and parish churches, the whole of that English scene which had made up so much of my life; and when I reached the top of the Berkshire Downs above Wantage, the burden of my fear of Rome seemed to fall from me. I decided that Hooker's view of the Church was as near to the truth as I could come, and that I would make my peace with the Church of England.

CHAPTER SIX

CONFLICT

I returned home with the intention of preparing myself for taking orders in the Church of England and I was advised to go and stay at the Oxford Mission in Bethnal Green to get some practical experience of work in the slums. This decision cost me more than any previous decision of my life. I had still deeply ingrained in me my prejudice against any form of ecclesiasticism and especially of the clerical life, but I realised that it was the test of my faith, if I really believed in the Church, to submit myself to its discipline, and the idea of work in the East End of London appealed to me. To my mother this was the cause of the greatest joy. She had always had a special affection for me, which I had returned at first quite spontaneously, taking pleasure in helping her in the house and confiding all my ambitions to her. Now that I had begun to think as a Christian, this bond was strengthened not only by my own feelings of the duty and love which were due to her, but also by our common feeling for religion. I used always to go to Communion with her and the thought of my taking orders was her highest ambition for me.

No doubt, this had a considerable effect on my decision to settle in the Church of England, but I was not allowed to rest long in this state of mind. I read some of Archbishop Laud's writings, in particular his controversy with Fisher, the Jesuit, and on the whole I think I considered that he had the best of the argument. I also learned more of the sacramental doctrine of the Church and of the idea of the Real Presence, though I never found anything more satisfactory than I had learned from Hooker. I also studied Bishop Butler's *Analogy of Religion* which made a deep impression on me, and I was much taken with the mystical works of William Law. This was, I think, the first time that I encountered any mystical doctrine, and it had a powerful effect on me. Law was a disciple of the German mystic, Jacob Boehme, and brought into the Church of England a current of mystical teaching which, though not precisely orthodox, was of great power and beauty, and saved the Church in the eighteenth century from succumbing to the universal spirit of rationalism. Though Bishop Butler's sane rationalism appealed to me, Law answered to a deeper need of my soul, of which I was now becoming conscious.

I had continued at home to keep up the practice of saying Morning and Evening Prayer every day and I tried to live as strict and regular a life as possible. But I found that the difficulty of adjusting myself to the normal round of life was immense. I had a strong inclination now to fasting. I found that when I fasted my brain became clear and my prayer gained in fervour and intensity, but the moment I relaxed everything began to fall away from me. My mother did not interfere, but many of my friends tried to dissuade me from it, and it became a constant burden to me. I felt that if I abandoned it, I was giving up all my hard-won faith, while if I continued I felt myself becoming more and more isolated from other people. I found in William Law and the High Church tradition for which he stood a justification for my practice and this encouraged me to continue, but it caused an almost intolerable conflict. My reason counselled me often to give way, especially as I began to grow incredibly thin and weak, but at the same time I felt a constant renewal of spiritual power and a deep longing for prayer which increased from day to day.

Often I would take long bicycle rides of sixty or eighty miles, as I still refused to go anywhere by train, and in the course of these rides I went through astounding experiences. I would usually stop for some bread and cheese and

beer at midday, but otherwise I tried to do without food.
Towards the end of the day, however, I often found myself
getting tired out and would be tempted to stop and take
some tea. This would often raise an appalling conflict in
my mind between reason and common sense on the one
hand, and the spirit of prayer and faith on the other hand :
but I found that if I resisted the temptation it often brought
with it a renewal of strength, both physical and spiritual,
which seemed almost miraculous. Thus I was strengthened
in my determination to continue.

If the conflict at home in the country was considerable,
when I came to London and settled at Bethnal Green, it
became intolerable. I now felt the full weight of that
world which I had rejected pressing upon me. The life of
prayer and austerity which I had been leading had increased my sensibility to an extreme degree, and I felt the
presence of the surrounding world as a violent oppression.
It was not simply a matter of sensibility. The life around
Bethnal Green among the poor and in the open market
attracted me; I felt that here was the human world which I
loved; and the vegetables displayed in the stalls in the
market made me feel the contact with the earth and the
country. But my mind had grown so deeply antagonistic to
the whole civilisation for which London stood that it filled
me with horror. I felt it as a giant force opposed to all that
I loved, ceaselessly beating against the doors of my mind,
breaking down my resistance and driving out the spirit of
prayer. I had read with deep conviction when I was at
home the words of St John : " Love not the world, nor the
things that are in the world. If any man love the world,
the love of the Father is not in him. For all that is in the
world, the lust of the flesh, the lust of the eyes and the pride
of life, is not of the Father, but of the world. And the
world passeth away with the lust thereof, but he that doeth
the will of God abideth for ever." These words had sunk
into my soul, and now I felt this "world" around me, the

world of time and flux and change and sensation, and I knew that it was at war with the world of that eternal order in which I believed.

I went to St Paul's Cathedral and Westminster Abbey, the British Museum and the National Gallery, to try to recover my sense of these eternal values, but nothing could give me any peace. I attended services also at Anglo-Catholic churches, and there I felt some sense of continuity with the past, but it was like a small island in a flood : the deep unrest in my soul remained. At last this sense of unrest came to a head. I had bought a book of Bishop Ken, one of the " non-juring " bishops of the seventeenth century who stood for the pure tradition of the Church of England, and in it I read some words about the need for repentance. Up to this time my religion had been to some extent external. I had engaged my mind and imagination, my feelings and my will, but it had never really touched my heart. Behind all my fervour and enthusiasm there had been an intense egoism. I acknowledged no real authority over myself. My religion was based on my own reason and my own will, and though I had come theoretically to accept the authority of the Church, it had no real effect on me.

Now for the first time I felt an overwhelming need to repent. I did not clearly understand what repentance was, nor was I aware of any particular sin of which I had to repent. It was simply that the unrest in my soul had turned from discontent with the world to a feeling of discontent with myself. There was nothing conscious or deliberate about it; it came to me as a command, and I kept saying to myself, scarcely knowing the meaning of what I said : " I must repent, I must repent." I went up in this state of mind to a small chapel at the top of the house one evening, and there, as I prayed, a resolution formed itself in my mind that I would not go to bed that night but would spend the whole night in prayer. Again the resolution seemed not to come from my own volition; it was an instinct with the force of a command.

I went, therefore, to my room and began to pray kneeling on the floor beside the bed, and immediately a furious conflict started in my mind. Reason and common sense told me that it was absurd to behave in this way. Beneath my unconventional behaviour, in many ways I was still deeply conventional, and I dreaded what people might think of me. Although I affected to despise the world, I was in fact still governed by its standards, and the idea of staying up all night in prayer appeared to me utterly absurd. I was also frightened of the isolation into which I felt that I was being driven. I had no real contact with anyone in London, and the people with whom I was staying, though good and kind, would have had no understanding of the conflict in my mind. I felt myself to be utterly alone in this vast city and I could find no human justification for what I was doing.

However, these were comparatively external considerations; what really terrified me was the conflict with my own reason. Until this time my reason and instinct had always gone hand in hand. My first experience of the beauty and mystery of nature had been confirmed by my reading of the poets and then of the philosophers. My discovery of Christianity had also gone on rational lines; at each stage I had seemed to find the book which I needed to satisfy both my reason and my instinct for beauty and holiness. Even my prayer had been perfectly rational and had been satisfied by the ordered beauty of the Book of Common Prayer, but now something irrational seemed to be coming into my life. There had been the desire for fasting which, though I might justify it by reason to some extent, came upon me as an irrational impulse; and now this call to repentance had come, as an apparently irrational urge, and my reason rose up against it. Which was I to obey, this obscure instinct, this apparently irrational urge, or my reason and common sense? The conflict was the most intense that I had ever endured, and it was part of the terms of the conflict, that it could not be answered by reason, because it was precisely the place of reason in my life which was in question.

The conflict went deeper than I could possibly understand. I had lived up till now by my own will. I had worked out my own philosophy and religion for myself and without knowing it I had made a God of my own reason. I had made myself the judge of everything in heaven and earth, and I acknowledged no power or authority over me. Even if theoretically I now acknowledged the authority of God and the Church, in practice I was still the ruler and the judge. I was the centre of my own existence, and my isolation from the rest of the world was due to the fact that I had deliberately shut myself up within the barriers of my own will and reason. Now I was being summoned to surrender this independence. Something had arisen in the depths of my own nature which my reason was powerless to control. I was being called to surrender the very citadel of my self. I was completely in the dark. I did not really know what repentance was or what I was required to repent of. It was this darkness which really made me afraid. Is not this the one thing of which we are all afraid? The darkness which is outside the sphere of our consciousness, the abyss where all known landmarks fail? This was what I was really facing and it was this which filled me with such unspeakable horror. I do not wish to exaggerate the nature of this ordeal, but it was indeed the turning point of my life. The struggle went on for many hours, but I realised at length that it was my reason which I had to renounce. My reason was the serpent which was threatening to devour my life. It was not merely the reason of convention and common sense, but the very autonomy of my reason which I was required to sacrifice. I had to surrender myself into the hands of a power which was above my reason, which would not allow me to argue, but commanded me to obey. Yet this power presented itself as nothing but darkness, as an utter blank.

In this state of mind I had but one resource. I had never been in the habit of meditating on the passion of Christ, but the scene in the Garden of Gethsemane had impressed itself on my imagination. I had always felt that in those hours Christ had faced the utter darkness of death and dereliction, the full tide of the power of evil sweeping over the world. Now I felt that this hour had come upon me, and I could only place myself beside him in the Garden of Gethsemane and wait for the night to pass. Once I had made up my mind not to listen to reason, the conflict ceased. It was only a matter of enduring to the end. So I set myself to remain kneeling on the floor, fighting against sleep and keeping my mind fixed on the figure of Christ. Somehow I managed to endure until it was morning. When I rose, I felt worn out and hopeless; I did not know what was to become of me. I did not feel that I could stay where I was and nothing else offered itself to me.

But as I was leaving my room, I suddenly heard a voice say: "You must go to a retreat." When I say that I heard a voice, I do not mean that I heard any sound. It was simply that this was signified to me interiorly, but in such a way that it did not appear to come from myself. I believe that I had heard the word "retreat" used once, but I am certain that I did not know what it meant. I associated it, I think, with some kind of clerical conference which I had heard of taking place in the country. The message came to me as a direct inspiration, though I did not know what it signified. I went, therefore, to an Anglo-Catholic church nearby and asked the priest if there was such a thing as a retreat to which I could go. He thought for a minute and then said: "Yes, there is one beginning this morning at Westminster House." The retreat was for a group of ordinands, but he thought that it would be possible for me to attend it. I went round to Westminster House which I found to be a house of the Cowley Fathers.

It is difficult to describe what happened when I reached

there. The retreat conferences were given by an old priest called Father Tovey. They were very simple in character and dealt with the fundamental doctrines of Original Sin and Redemption, of the Incarnation and the Holy Trinity. This was the first time that I had ever heard these doctrines expounded in a way which had any meaning to me. He based himself on St Thomas, which I recognised with pleasure, but he gave them a living personal application which touched my heart. I had studied philosophy and theology, and I knew the elements of church history and church doctrine, but the simple truth of the faith had never before been set before me. Now it penetrated my soul in such a way that I was appalled to think that I had never understood it before. I had rejected the Church and gone my own way, working out my religion for myself, and here all the time the truth had been among the people I had despised. My whole life seemed to have been one gigantic mistake. I had turned my back on the truth, and sought it blindly in the opposite direction, and now I had been forced back to the point from which I started.

The repentance for which I had blindly asked the night before now came over me like a flood. I went to confession for the first time in my life and tears poured from my eyes, tears of a kind which I had never known before. My whole being seemed to be renewed. When I went into the church and heard the chanting of the Psalms, it seemed that the words were being spoken in the depths of my own soul and were the utterances of my own prayer. They were chanting the 119th Psalm; it must have been in plainchant, though I did not know it, and no doubt this must have stirred my soul, for there is no music on earth like it; but it was the words which engraved themselves on my mind:

Blessed are those that are undefiled in the way: and walk in the law of the Lord.
Blessed are they that keep his testimonies and seek him with their whole heart. . . .

With my whole heart have I sought thee : O let me not
go wrong out of thy commandments. . . .
Open thou my eyes that I may see the wondrous things
of thy law.

I had come through the darkness into a world of light.
That eternal truth and beauty which the sights and sounds
of London threatened to banish from my sight was here
the universal law. I heard its voice sounding in my ears.
The very stones of the house seemed to be the living stones
of a temple in which this song ascended. It was as though I
had been given a new power of vision. Everything seemed
to lose its hardness and rigidity and to become alive. When
I looked at the crucifix on the wall, the figure on it seemed
to be a living person; I felt that I was in the house of God.
When I went outside I found that the world about me no
longer oppressed me as it had done. The hard casing of
exterior reality seemed to have been broken through, and
everything disclosed its inner being. The buses in the
street seemed to have lost their solidity and to be glowing
with light. I hardly felt the ground as I trod, and I think
that I must have been in some danger of being run over.
I was like a bird which has broken the shell of its egg and
finds itself in a new world; like a child who has forced its
way out of the womb and sees the light of day for the first
time.

When I returned to the house I went to my room and
took up the New Testament. There I read the words of
St John : "Not that we loved God, but that He loved us",
and suddenly the meaning of what had happened dawned
on my mind. Through all these years I had thought that
I had been seeking God. The presence which had appeared
to me beneath the forms of nature that day at school; the
beauty which I had found in the poets; the truth which
philosophy had opened to me; and finally the revelation of
Christianity; all these had seemed to be steps on my way of
ascent towards God. Now I suddenly saw that all the time

it was not I who had been seeking God, but God who had been seeking me. I had made myself the centre of my own existence and had my back turned to God. All the beauty and truth which I had discovered had come to me as a reflection of his beauty, but I had kept my eyes fixed on the reflection and was always looking at myself. But God had brought me to the point at which I was compelled to turn away from the reflection, both of myself and of the world which could only mirror my own image. During that night the mirror had been broken, and I had felt abandoned because I could no longer gaze upon the image of my own reason and the finite world which it knew. God had brought me to my knees and made me acknowledge my own nothingness, and out of that knowledge I had been reborn. I was no longer the centre of my life and therefore I could see God in everything.

That night before I went to bed I opened a book by St John of the Cross and read in it the words : " I will lead thee by a way thou knowest not to the secret chamber of love." The words struck home to me as though they had been spoken to me. Though I had never been without affection for my family and had had many friends, yet I had never till this moment really known the meaning of love. My strongest feelings had gone into my love for nature and for poetry. Yet always I had had the feeling that in love the secret of life was to be found. And now I felt that love take possession of my soul. It was as though a wave of love flowed over me, a love as real and personal as any human love could be, and yet infinitely transcending all human limitations. It invaded my being and seemed to fill not only my soul but also my body. My body seemed to dissolve, as things about me had done, and felt light and buoyant. When I lay down I felt as though I might float on the bed, and I experienced such rapture that I could imagine no ecstasy of love beyond it.

During the retreat Father Tovey had compared the action of grace to a small child standing over an open trap-

door into a cellar where his father is standing. The cellar
is in darkness and the child can see nothing. But he knows
that his father is there, and his father tells him to jump.
That is what had happened to me; I had jumped into the
darkness, and I had been caught in the arms of love.

When I returned home after this, I thought that all my
troubles were over. But I found that they had only increased. The old passion for fasting returned to me in
greater force than ever, and now a new trial was added.
Whenever I tried to go to bed, the thought would come to
me that I ought to stay up in prayer. I seemed to see the
darkness opening up in front of me again, and something
seemed to urge me to cast myself into it. But I drew back
in fear. I was still terrified of doing anything that might be
thought unbalanced, and I feared the exhaustion which
would follow on a long night's vigil. If I did lie down, then
I felt that I ought to lie on the floor, and I had a sense of
guilt lying in bed.

When I read the lives of the saints, which I now began
to do, I found that these practices of fasting and watching
had been habitual with them, but no one now seemed to
countenance them. I went to the Cowley Fathers at Oxford
to try to obtain some help and advice, but I received none
that was of any use. At last I decided that I must give up
these practices and try to live as other people. But though
the conflict in my mind was resolved for the time being, I
was immediately overcome by other trials. I found that the
Bible began to lose its meaning for me. I was still in the
habit of reading a portion every day, and as long as I lived
a strict life of fasting and sacrifice, the words came to me
charged with meaning and spoke to my soul. But as soon
as I gave up fasting, they seemed to lose their meaning, and
I felt my faith beginning to give way. I became uncertain
as to what I really believed.

At Cowley I had come in contact with Anglo-Catholicism
in a form which touched my heart; I had felt that there if
anywhere was the living Church of Christ. I had dis-

covered the Divine Office and the religious life. I had
learned the meaning of the crucifix, which I had never
seen used before. At Newbury I went to the Anglo-Catholic
church, and I felt myself at home there. But I asked myself
what was the relation of Anglo-Catholicism to the Church
of England. Was it the true doctrine of the Church, and if
so what was the place of Protestantism? At Cowley I had
been astonished to find a commentary on the Exercises of
St Ignatius. I thought at first that it must be St Ignatius
of Antioch, one of the early Apostolic Fathers, but I found
that it was indeed St Ignatius of Loyola. What then was
the relation of Anglo-Catholicism to the Church of Rome?
Curiously enough, I do not think that I gave any serious
consideration to the Roman Church; it was simply the doctrine of the Church of England which concerned me. I was
faced with the problem above all in the matter of communion. What was the true nature of the sacrament? Was
it the Body of Christ, or was Christ merely present in it in
some undefined way, or was it simply bread and wine which
faith made into a means of communion with Christ? I
knew that all these different views were held in the Church
of England and that there was no one who could tell me
which was true.

Now that both the Bible and the Church had begun to
fail me, I turned to the mystics, and in them I found some
help. After I had left the Cowley Fathers the glow of
feeling had remained with me for some time, and when it
faded I was left with a permanent sense of the presence of
God in everything which I saw and heard. I felt it when I
lay down to sleep and when I awoke in the morning and at
every hour of the day. It was so strong upon me that I was
in danger of leaving myself to divine guidance for the
smallest thing. I did not seem so much to act for myself
as to let an unseen power act within me. All that I read in
the mystics, especially the German mystics, Tauler and
Suso, but also the less orthodox Spiritual Guide of the
Spaniard da Molinos, encouraged me to believe that the

presence which I now felt habitually in the depths of my soul was indeed the presence of God; it had no form but was rather a "dazzling darkness", as Henry Vaughan described it, in which I felt the abyss of God's being was contained. But this sense of infinite power and love about me made it almost impossible for me to make decisions for myself. I wanted to abandon myself utterly to this power, and I did not know how to decide to think and act for myself. Thus the need for some guide, some authority on which I could rely became ever more pressing. I even went on to read again some of the Hindu and Buddhist mystics which I had studied in the past, and I began to doubt exactly what I believed about God. Was He truly a Person, as Christian writers maintained, or might He not be conceived impersonally, like Brahma, or again might not the absolute reality be simply a state, like the Nirvana of the Buddha?

Thus my mind was gradually reduced to chaos. All the elements of religion which had been building up into a living structure in my soul, and had seemed to meet in the harmony of a living temple, of which Christ was the cornerstone and the principle of unity, now fell apart, and I was lost in confusion. At last I decided that I must make a new start.

I had been reading the life of St Anthony, the first hermit of the Egyptian desert, and also the letters of St Basil and his brother, St Gregory of Nazianzum, and their example suggested a way of escape from my dilemma. I was especially attracted by St Basil and St Gregory, because they had been university students together at Athens and I felt a kinship with them. They spoke a language which I could understand; they had been students of Greek philosophy and had deliberately renounced the world for the solitude of the country.

I decided that I would follow their example. I remembered a place which I had seen on my walks in the Cotswolds, where there was a signpost pointing up a glen towards what the postman had told me was a lonely, desolate spot away on the hills, to which no one ever came. I decided that this was the place for a hermitage, and that I would put my trust in God and go there. My intention was to lead a life of prayer and meditation, taking my Bible and a few books with me, in the hope that God would reveal his will to me. St Basil had said that bread and water and any fruit and vegetables that could be obtained were sufficient for food, and I trusted that I would be able to get these. So I put all my worldly possessions in a knapsack and set off with this on my back. As I left home, I turned to look back on it and I had a feeling that I was leaving it for ever.

CHAPTER SEVEN

ALONE WITH THE ALONE

Returning to the Cotswolds, I soon found the signpost which I had remembered and took the road through a glen with wooded hills rising on either side. After walking for about a mile I came to a little thatched cottage by the side of a wood, which seemed to have been built for a hermitage. When I reached the farm which was about half a mile beyond, I learned to my grief that it had been let that very day, but I was told that there were some cottages lying still farther up the valley, and that one of them was empty. I went on up with the farmer. The woods had now given place to open pasture on which sheep were grazing, and after a few minutes, right at the top of the valley, about nine hundred feet up, there appeared a group of farm buildings protected by a belt of trees.

I found that the cottage was all that I desired. It was a plain, two-roomed cottage attached to another similar cottage where a farm labourer was living with his wife and children. This was fortunate for me as they agreed to provide me with all necessary food and to do my washing. I agreed with the farmer to take the cottage immediately, and wrote to Martyn to ask him to bring over the bed and straw mattress which I had had at Eastington. I then bought myself a sleeping bag, a table, a stool and a clock, and with these I took up my residence.

I had the *Summa* of St Thomas with me and a few volumes of the Fathers and my old Gothic Bible. I also hung up a crucifix over the table; I had no other furniture. There was a kitchen downstairs which I used as a wash room, as I was determined not to do any cooking. I lived entirely in the room upstairs, which was a big room with just bare boards and rafters, but warm and water-tight. There was no heating or lighting; the water came from a tap in the garden and there was an earth-closet as at Eastington. I arranged to have some cooked vegetables at midday, but otherwise I decided to live on bread and milk and any dried fruit I could get.

It would have been all right, perhaps, if I could have stuck to this arrangement, but my passion for fasting attacked me again more than ever. I could not fix on any rule of life which would satisfy me. I tried to arrange my life in periods of two hours, giving two hours to prayer, then two to reading and meditation, and two to walking or other recreation. But I could not be satisfied with this. I began to think that the cooked meal was unnecessary and tried to live on bread and milk and dried fruit alone. I also cut the recreation down to a walk in the afternoon. But the most serious difficulty was over prayer. I found that the more I prayed, the stronger the inclination grew. Again I was tempted to stay up all night in prayer, and once or twice I did so, but the fear of becoming unbalanced tormented me. The urge to pray was overwhelming; sometimes it seemed that all the powers of heaven were drawing me and the whole world appeared transfigured. The Bible recovered all its old meaning and I would read it for hours on end. I seemed to be on the verge of a great revelation, but then the reaction would set in and I would grow afraid.

The only time I went far afield was on Sunday when I walked the four miles down the hill to Winchcombe and received Communion. I always went fasting and returned tired after the long walk up the hill, but I got great happiness from it. Otherwise, my walks were on the hills around. There were no proper roads, but only farm roads and cart tracks, and I had practically the whole world to myself. I went down each day to the farm to get my milk but otherwise I had very little contact with anyone. I must have lived between two and three months in this way, trying one thing and then another, and never finding any peace. At last I was reduced to despair and began to think that the whole experiment had been a failure. So I wrote to Martyn again and asked him to come and fetch me and my belongings away.

But no sooner had I posted the letter than I began to feel disturbed by what I had done. I had come there to live in answer to what I believed to be a call from God, and now I felt that I had betrayed my trust and lost my opportunity. I went to bed in great distress of mind, and as soon as I rose in the morning, I began to think what I could do. Then it came into my mind that I must turn to God and find out His will at whatever cost. I realised that I must make up my mind whether I was going to live according to the judgment of the world or according to my faith in God. I had felt the power of God in my life. From the moment when that revelation came to me at school, I felt that I had been led by a definite providence. I had come to believe in God as a Father to whom the " hairs of our head are all numbered ". I believed that He had spoken to Abraham, Isaac and Jacob, to Moses and the Prophets. I believed in Christ as the Son of the Father. I believed in the Church which he had founded, and that he had promised to be with his disciples till the end of the world. I determined now once and for all to put my life in His hands and to trust to Him alone.

Up till this time there had always been a reserve in my prayer. I was performing an exercise which I would continue for a certain time. Now I determined to do what an obscure impulse had been urging me to do all the time, to pray without reserve, and not to rise from my knees until I had received an answer. I shut myself in a little closet which opened out of the room, where there was only a skylight, in order that I might be more completely shut off from the world. Then I placed myself in imagination at the foot of the cross and began to pray with all my strength. Immediately I seemed to be carried away by a great wave of prayer, and I lost consciousness of everything else.

Almost immediately it seemed that an answer came. It was something so simple, that it is a wonder that I had not thought of it before. But it came to me as an inspiration from heaven and it brought complete peace to my mind. I saw that I must not try to live as I had been doing, but to take work on the farm and work out my purpose in this way. This was revealed to me with perfect clarity and certainty and I rose from my knees feeling fully assured.

I went to write another letter to Martyn asking him not to come, and as I did so I looked at the clock. When I had begun to pray it had been about eight o'clock in the morning and I thought that I had been praying for perhaps two hours. But I found that it was four o'clock in the afternoon and I had only just time to catch the post. To this day I do not know what happened to me during those hours. I was completely unconscious of the passage of time, and my mind had been totally absorbed in prayer. But something happened to me then in the depths of my soul which determined the rest of my life.

During most of our waking hours we live on the surface of our being in contact with all the different things which are presented to our senses. Sometimes when we are deep in conversation with a friend or reading a book or perhaps in a dangerous situation, we lose the sense of time and enter into a deeper region of the soul, where it is withdrawn from the outer world : but we are still not far from the surface. Beyond this, beyond all thought and feeling and imagination, there is an inner sanctuary into which we scarcely ever enter. It is the ground or substance of the soul, where all the faculties have their roots, and which is the very centre of our being. It is here that the soul is at all times in direct contact with God. For behind all the phenomena of the world, behind the sights and sounds, behind the forms and energies of nature, there is the ever active presence of God, which sustains them in their being and moves them to act. It was into this region that I believe I was drawn at this time, and my will in the silent depths of its being reached out to the will of God.

All that I had been through up till this hour had been leading up to this. At Eastington I had been led through the asceticism, which our way of life forced on us, to break with the material world and to control my natural feelings and appetites. Then in the painful struggle in prayer during the night with the Cowley Fathers, I had been brought to renounce my own reason. Now I was made to renounce my own will, to surrender the inmost centre of my being. Each renunciation had been dragged out of me painfully against my own will. I had struggled against it and felt it as an invasion of my being by an alien power. There was indeed something terrifying in this power which had entered into my life and which would not be refused. It had revealed itself to me as love, but I knew now that it was a love which demanded everything, and which was a torment if it was resisted. Once the surrender had been made, that power took over the direction of my life. I had been striving to come to terms with it, to allot it a certain place in my life but it had shown me that it would accept no compromise. I had wanted to keep my own will and to direct my own life; but now I had been forced to surrender. I had placed my life in the hands of a power which was infinitely beyond me and I knew from this time that the sole purpose of my life must be to leave myself in those hands and to allow my soul to be governed by that will.

I could never doubt after this that behind all the accidents of this life, behind all the pain and the conflict, there was a definite power at work which was shaping human destiny. The pain and the conflict arose from the resistance of the human will to this power, and this resistance in turn was due to our blindness. We were held captive by the material world, the world of reason and common sense; only when we had broken with the illusion of this world and faced the reality which was hidden in the depths of our being could we find peace.

For myself everything was now changed. I took work on the farm the next day and had my meals now at the farm house together with the farmer and his wife and their three children and Ted, the shepherd. It was a lonely life for these people. The children used to go off to school every day to the little village about three miles away, and the farmer and his wife used to go by car to Cheltenham every Saturday, but otherwise we lived a life apart in the regular routine of the farm. I used to help with the milking every morning before breakfast, and after breakfast I usually went the round of the sheep with Ted. It was a big farm of about eight hundred acres and it would take us a good part of the morning to climb the hills and seek out all the sheep. Sometimes a ewe would have gone astray in one of the thickets and we might spend the whole of the morning looking for her.

In this way I was often reminded of the Gospels and my life began to fall into that pattern in which the Bible had always meant so much to me. Ted was a Welshman who read his Bible in Welsh, and felt the religious background of a shepherd's life no less than I did. The life was often hard, though, especially as winter drew on. Sometimes a cloud would cover the hilltops and one would have to go searching for the cows to bring them back to milk in the evening in a thick mist. I shall never forget, also, topping the turnips in a frost, when the cold cut like a knife and one had to make an effort each time to take hold of the top. But it was the life which I needed above everything. I felt that I was part once more of a human family and my mind regained its normal balance.

In the meantime, as it was now September, I bought myself an oil stove and every evening I returned to my cottage to read. I used to go down to Winchcombe whenever I had an afternoon free and buy books, and I renewed my friendship with Michael Cardew. One day when I was sitting in my room, he rode up on horseback with a girl who was working with him in the pottery, whose name was Barbara Millard. She was a South African, who had been brought up in the wilds of Southern Rhodesia, and we immediately became friends. She shared all my love for the open country and we used to take long walks together in the hills, sometimes taking our lunch and spending the whole days together over the weekend. She was religious by nature and we used to go together to Communion at the church at Winchcombe; but like most people she had her difficulties in regard to the Church of England and we spent many hours discussing them. I think that this was the only time that the idea of marriage ever entered into my mind; but it was really a relation of friendship not of love, and our ways soon divided. She went back to South Africa soon afterwards and married. I heard from her regularly for two or three years, and then I received a letter from her husband telling me that she had been killed in a fall from her horse. When we parted I told her that even if we should never meet again in this world, I should never feel really separated from her, and I think that I realised then for the first time the true nature of a friendship which is founded on the love of God, and which unites two people in such a way that even death cannot divide them.

My own way lay in a different direction. I began to read again without much definite purpose, and I bought three books, The *Journal* of George Fox, the *Autobiography* of Richard Baxter and the *Diary* of John Woolman, the Quaker. I discovered then a new aspect of that seventeenth century which I had always loved, the tradition of non-conformity. I felt again the wonderful strength of the religious spirit in seventeenth-century England and this new aspect appealed to me in its own way no less than the Anglicanism of Hooker and Jeremy Taylor. I do not know exactly what conception of the Church I had at this time, but I think that I would have regarded the Quakers and Congregationalists, no less than the Anglicans and Orthodox and Catholics, as all alike members of the one mystical Body of Christ, though differing in their forms of worship and belief.

It happened that shortly after this I saw an advertisement in a catalogue of Newman's *Development of Christian Doctrine,* which I proceeded to buy. I do not think that my mind had ever seriously returned to the thought of the Roman Church, and I bought the book simply out of general interest, but its effect on me was to prove decisive. I had always felt a deep sympathy with Newman. His approach to the Church by way of the Bible and the Fathers and the High Church party had been that which I had followed. Now I found Newman turning all his learning and all his powers of exegesis to showing that the Church of the Scriptures and the Fathers was none other than the Church of Rome. Newman's method also appealed to me; I had always been interested in the historical approach. I believed that the Church which Christ had founded was a historical reality, that it had had a continuous history from the time of the Apostles to the present day. I had thought that this continuity might be found in the Church of England, but now the overwhelming weight of evidence for the continuity of the Roman Church was presented to my mind.

The problem was how could one reconcile all the developments which have taken place in the Church of Rome with the primitive simplicity of the Gospel. What was the connection between the religion of the Gospels and the complete structure of Catholicism as seen, for instance, in Dante or St Thomas or a Gothic cathedral? That the religion of Dante and St Thomas was a corruption of the Gospel I could not believe. The polemic of the Reformation had ceased to have any meaning for me. I knew that it was the modern world which was corrupt and decadent, and that Dante and St Thomas marked one of the pinnacles of human greatness.

How then could one reconcile the vast elaboration of

dogma and ritual and what looked like mythology in the Middle Ages with the original Gospel? Newman gave me the answer, an answer which accorded with everything which I knew from other sources. He saw the Church as a living organism, beginning like a seed in the New Testament and gradually developing according to specific laws until it reached its full stature. Now this view accorded perfectly with that view of the Church as the Mystical Body of Christ which had impressed itself on my imagination when I first read St Paul. St Paul had compared the Church to a human body composed of many organs, but all subject to one head and animated by one spirit. Thus the idea of the Church as a living organism was clearly part of the teaching of the New Testament. Again Christ himself had spoken of his Kingdom as a grain of mustard seed, which beginning very small gradually grows to be a great tree so that the birds of heaven come to rest among its branches. Here then was the authority of the Gospel itself for this gradual organic development of the Church from small beginnings to a great stature.

This principle accorded also with all that was known of the processes of nature and history. Newman's book had been written a few years before Darwin's *Origin of Species,* when the conception of organic development was first applied on a large scale to the structure of living beings. Every species in nature was seen to develop gradually from small beginnings, adapting itself to new conditions and assimilating elements from outside, and yet preserving its essential type. These developments could only be explained on the assumption that there was an inner principle of growth in an organism which enabled it to select those elements which were favourable to it and to reject those which were hostile, and so to perfect its species. It was evident also that there were false developments, failures in adaptation, which resulted in the corruption of a species and its gradual extinction.

I had also been familiar, ever since I had read Spengler,

with the application of this principle to human history. I had seen how human civilisations have their rise and fall, and how this can be seen to depend on the development of certain principles of growth and corruption inherent in them. Thus, everything disposed me in favour of Newman's view of the growth of the Church. But it was the particular application of this theory to individual doctrines which really convinced me. Newman showed how every Christian doctrine had undergone this process of development. It was not a matter of certain doctrines which were peculiar to the Church of Rome : the most fundamental doctrines of the Trinity and the Incarnation had undergone a similar development. I had often been disturbed by the Athanasian Creed with its apparent imposition of the most complex theological dogma on the simple doctrine of the New Testament, but now I could see the reason for it. Newman supported me in my belief that the New Testament was addressed to the Imagination. It was first of all a record of facts, which were presented to the mind in the most vivid, imaginative way. It was a poetic history, and, in addition, the doctrine of the New Testament was presented entirely in imaginative terms. There were no abstract philosophical concepts; all was expressed in the richly symbolic terms of poetry and imagination. Christ spoke of himself in terms of the Messiah and his Kingdom, two concepts of infinite imaginative significance. He compared himself to a Bridegroom, to a Shepherd, to a Vine. Even the terms in which he spoke of his relation to God were profoundly symbolic; he spoke of God as his Father, of himself as the Son, of the Spirit which he would send. Now these terms set forth the Object of faith, as Newman showed, in the way which makes the deepest impression on the mind and nourishes love and devotion, but they are lacking in precision. It was inevitable that as the minds of men began to reflect on them and to draw out their meaning, they should be given a more exact expression. In Newman's own words, "what was an impression on the imagination became a system or creed in the reason ".

Thus the development of theology was like the development of any other science. It was simply the application of an exact philosophic reason to the evidence of the New Testament. The whole weight of Greek philosophy was gradually brought to bear on the revelation of the New Testament, and the *Summa* of St Thomas was the organised structure of human thought working on the material provided by the original revelation. But what was to show that this was a genuine development and not a corruption of the Gospel? Here Newman showed that as the Church was the Body of which Christ was the Head, so it was necessarily guided and directed in the course of its evolution by his Spirit. The Church as the organ of divine revelation, founded by Christ and inspired by his Spirit, was necessarily infallible in its teaching. It was simply the organism through which the divine message was communicated to men, and therefore it was always preserved in truth. The idea that the Church was infallible had long been familiar to me. I saw clearly that it could have no authority to teach in Christ's name if this was not so.

Where did this infallible authority reside in the Church? I knew that in the early Church it was held to reside in the Bishops. Some time ago I had bought Archbishop Wake's translation of the works of the Apostolic Fathers, and this had created a great impression on me. I had often wondered what was the link between the Church of the Apostles, as it is seen in the New Testament, and the Church of later times, and these letters of the Apostolic Fathers had provided the answer to my question. They were the immediate successors of the Apostles, and they showed what the Church was like at the end of the first and the beginning of the second century. St Ignatius of Antioch in particular revealed that the Bishop at this time had taken the place of the Apostles. The bishop was the representative of Christ in each individual church. Each church formed as it were a cell in the Mystical Body of Christ. It was an organic unit, modelled on the pattern of the whole, and the bishop as the head occupied the position of Christ. It was through him that the teaching of Christ was given to the people; "the bishops were sent by the Apostles, the Apostles by Christ, Christ by God", as an early writer had put it.

It was clear, then, that the infallible guidance in the teaching of the Church came through the bishops, and this I knew was the universal belief of the early Church. Among these bishops the Bishop of Rome was held to have a unique position because he was the successor of St Peter. I do not think that I had ever studied this question before, but Newman was able to show me that this doctrine was no less universal in the early Church. Christ had founded his Church on St Peter and given him the supreme authority over it, symbolised by the "keys", like the power of a steward over a house. I saw now that in the organisation of the Church, as it spread throughout the Roman Empire, the Bishop of Rome as the successor of St Peter was held to have the same authority among the other bishops as St Peter held among the Apostles. As the bishop represented Christ in his own diocese and was head of the body of the Church there, so the Bishop of Rome represented Christ as head of the whole body of the Church throughout the world.

Newman showed how this doctrine could be seen developing step by step from the first words spoken by Christ to St Peter through the Fathers of the second and third centuries to the great Fathers of the fourth and fifth century, St Athanasius, St Ambrose, St Jerome, St Augustine. It was true that the doctrine had not always been clear from the beginning, but neither had the doctrine of the Trinity and the Incarnation, of Original Sin and Grace. The authority for holding each doctrine was precisely the same; it was the witness of the universal Church. In each case there had been a development, in the one case a theoretical development by the simple application of reason to the doctrine of the New Testament, in the other, a practical development also, as circumstances called for the exercise of the power of the Popes.

It was especially striking how the early Popes, far from resting their authority on any worldly power, regarded themselves as mystically identified with St Peter. Thus an early Pope could say : " We bear the burden of all who are laden; yea rather the blessed Peter beareth them in us, who as we trust in all things protects and defends us the heirs of his government." And again, St Leo could say : " Blessed Peter has not deserted the helm of the Church, which he had assumed . . . his power lives and his authority is pre-eminent in his See." It was clear that the sense of the Church as a living organism was so strong that St Peter was considered to continue to exercise his authority through the Pope, just as Christ himself continued to live and act in the Church in all its members.

What Newman showed of the Papal authority he showed also of all the other doctrines which were in dispute, of Purgatory and Indulgences, of the cultus of the Saints and their relics; all alike could be seen to be organic developments of the original doctrine of the Gospel, evolving by the same law as an oak tree develops from an acorn, or an embryo into a complete animal. Newman enumerated seven principles by which the genuineness of the development could be tested and distinguished from a corruption. They were the preservation of its type, the continuity of its principles, its power of assimilation, its logical sequence, its power to anticipate the future and to conserve the past, and finally its chronic vigour. Each of these tests was then scientifically applied to the doctrine of the Roman Church and it was shown how it had answered to the test. It would scarcely be possible to find a more rigorously scientific demonstration, but at the same time it was the work of a man who was not originally inclined to the view which he

was expounding and whose life depended on the result of
his investigations. When Newman began to write the
Development of Christian Doctrine, he was an Anglican;
when he had finished, he was a Catholic.

The effect of this argument on my mind was immense. It
corresponded in all its main principles with the lines on
which my mind had been previously working, while it
extended their range. It filled in all the gaps in my knowledge and gave a coherent meaning to everything I knew. I
had recognised the greatness of the medieval Church long
ago. I had seen how our civilisation had declined as it had
departed from those principles on which the medieval
world had been built. I had discovered in the Bible the
source of those principles and in the Church the society in
which they were to be found embodied. I knew that there
was no basis for life to be found in the world today apart
from the Church, and I had sought to find in the Church of
England the living representative of the Church which
Christ had founded. Now I saw that the living Church,
which could show a continuous evolution from the day of
Pentecost and whose doctrine had been built up through
successive centuries through the guidance of the indwelling
Spirit, was none other than the Church of Rome.

Here at last was the society which I had been seeking
which had stood out uncompromisingly against the illusions
of the modern world and preserved the tradition of the
past; here at last I could find a genuine basis for my life. I
began to realise now something of the significance of that
act of prayer which had changed my life. I had renounced
the world then with all the strength of my will, without seeing any alternative and trusting myself blindly to the hands
of God. Now God had answered my prayer in a way which
had been utterly beyond me. He had shown me the only
alternative to the world, to that civilisation which I knew
to be founded on false principles. He had shown me the
living Church, the Pillar and Ground of truth, the source
of life and salvation.

I thought all this out while I was working on the farm during the day, and returned each evening to my cottage to read more of Newman. I remember that we were topping turnips at the time, and as I went up and down the rows with the men I thought to myself that if ever my life had been sane and my mind calm it was now. I was free from all the distractions of the outside world. I was living a simple life in harmony with nature and among kindly practical people, unaffected by the sophistication of town life. There were no ties of emotion now to hold me back. I knew that I should give pain to my mother, but I repeated to myself again and again the text of the Gospel: "Unless a man will hate his father and his mother and his wife and his children, and his own life also, he cannot be my disciple." I knew that true love will never hesitate to give pain to those it loves when truth demands it and that my mother would not ask anything else.

It only remained for me to make contact with the Catholic Church. It will give some idea of the isolation in which I had lived, when I say that I did not know the name of a single Catholic to whom I could turn. My only resource was to go to my bookseller in Winchcombe and ask him if he knew whether there was such a thing as a Catholic church in the neighbourhood. He replied that there was one round the corner, and there I went. This time no obstacle presented itself. The priest was a Father Palmer, the son of an old English Catholic family, who told me proudly that he had nearly been sent to Christ's Hospital to school, but when his mother heard that it would be necessary for him to attend a Protestant service, she had replied that she would rather go to the workhouse with her eleven children than submit to that.

He understood my need and lent me two books by R. H. Benson, which exactly suited me. The first was *Christ in the Church,* which showed that the doctrine of the Mystical Body of Christ was indeed the doctrine of the Catholic Church: that as Christ had acted through his human nature while he was on earth, so now he acted through the organism of his Church, exercising his authority through her ministers, teaching the truth about her doctrine, saving souls through her sacraments. The other book was *The Friendship of Christ* which showed me how, while Christ continues to live and act through the social organism of the Church, he is none the less present to each individual soul, revealing himself as its friend and lover.

Thus all that I had come to believe was confirmed, but I still held back. I had been through so many phases of thought, that I felt that I could no longer trust my mind alone. I needed some further assurance that the Church was in fact the Body of Christ, and I remember that I wrote to my mother and told her that I would do nothing until I received this assurance that the Church was still today inhabited by the Spirit of Christ. I would wait until I received a positive assurance of the presence of Christ in the Church.

CHAPTER EIGHT

THE MONASTIC COMMUNITY

I had not long to wait. Soon after this Father Palmer said that he wished to take me over to a monastery in the neighbourhood. I do not think that I knew of the existence of any such things as a monastery at that time. I had often driven out to the old Cistercian abbey of Hailes near Winchcombe when I was at Oxford, and I had visited Rievaulx and Fountains and other medieval ruins; but they were simply relics of the past to me, and I had no idea that there were any existing in the modern world. The discovery, therefore, that there was a monastery actually within a few miles of Gloucester and Cheltenham came as a complete surprise. But as soon as I came there I knew that this was what I had unconsciously been seeking all these years. Even now after twenty years I can recall the impression which it first made on me. It was an experience almost as surprising as my first discovery of the beauty of nature at school. The natural setting was certainly as lovely as could be imagined. It was an old Cotswold manor house standing on the side of a hill, where the Cotswolds slope down to meet the plain. The country had none of the bare austerity of the hills above Northleach with their grim grey walls running across the windswept fields. Here the hills were covered with beeches and the fields were studded with trees like a park. In front lay the plain stretching to the Malvern hills in the distance and the tower of what had once been Gloucester Abbey rising up in the foreground as a silent witness to the religion which had once dominated the countryside.

It was not, however, the outward setting which now moved me. I discovered what had been the inner life of the cathedrals and monasteries which I had visited in the past. It was a beauty of a different kind from anything which I had known before, a beauty not of the natural but of the supernatural order. The presence of God had been revealed to me on that day at school beneath the forms of nature, the birds' song, the flowers' scent, the sunset over the fields; but now it was another presence which I perceived, the presence of God in the mystery not of nature but of Grace. Externally it was shown in the white habits of the monks, in the chant and ceremonies of the choir, in the order and dignity of the life which they led, and it was not long before I discovered the inner secret of the life. It was something which had been hidden from me all these years, something which I had been seeking without knowing exactly what it was, the secret of prayer.

Prayer had always been for me something private and apart, something of which one would never dream of speaking to anyone else. But now I found myself in an atmosphere where prayer was the breath of life. It was accepted as something as normal as eating and drinking. I shall never forget my surprise when someone told me quite casually that he would pray for me; the supernatural world suddenly became for me something positive and real, something quite matter-of-fact. I realised now what it was that I had missed all this time. It was the absence of prayer as a permanent background to life which made modern life so empty and meaningless. Life in the modern world was cut off from its source in God; men's minds were shut up in the confines of the material world and their own personalities, unable to escape from their fetters. Here the mind was kept open to God, and everything was brought into relation with Him. I had caught a glimpse of this with the Cowley Fathers in London, but now I saw it as an abiding reality which gave its meaning to life.

Prinknash Priory, as it then was, was a Benedictine monastery, which had been founded originally in the Church of England in an attempt to restore the monastic life to the Church of England. But after some years the community found it impossible to find any authority for their way of life in the Church of England, and were received into the Catholic Church. They lived for many years on the Island of Caldey off the coast of Wales, but in 1928 they moved to Prinknash Park, a property which had once belonged to the Abbots of Gloucester. There were about thirty monks in the community when I first came, and the Prior was Father Benedict Steuart. Later the community was raised to the rank of an Abbey, and grew in numbers to such an extent that it has now made two more foundations, one at Farnborough in Hampshire and one at Pluscarden Priory, the remains of a thirteenth-century monastery in Scotland.

Father Benedict received me with great kindness and I was invited to stay as long as I liked. I stayed for six weeks, and every day my conviction grew that here I had found the truth and the life which I was seeking. Father Benedict used to talk to me every day at coffee after dinner in the monastic refectory, and I found that he could answer all my questions. Even questions of sex, which I would not have dared to discuss with any clergyman before, I found were treated as easily and naturally as questions of prayer and theology.

I did not receive any formal instruction, and I think that Father Palmer was rather shocked when he came over later, to find that I had not even been through the Catechism. But I absorbed the faith at a deeper level than any provided by the Catechism. I attended the Offices in Church every day, and I found there the full extent of that prayer which I had begun to discover in the Book of Common Prayer in the Church of England. It began at four o'clock in the morning and extended throughout the day and gave me exactly what I had been looking for. The intervals I spent mostly in reading in the library, where I found all the books which I could possibly desire. In a very little time every lingering doubt was removed; here was the fullness of truth for which I had been seeking. I had found in the faith the key to all truth, and I realised that only now could I really begin to assimilate it.

But it was not only intellectual certainty which I desired; I wanted to find a life which would satisfy my whole being, my heart and soul and body as well as my mind. It was some time before I felt a complete conviction in regard to this. I saw that the life was based not only on prayer but also on work, and I got the impression that the work was taken seriously. All the work of the house was done by the monks and there were a garden and a farm and a carpenter's shop with many other kinds of workshop. Above all, I found a spirit of kindness and charity in the place such as I had never experienced before. I had been used to ordinary kindness and family affection, but I had never known a charity which was based on principle and pervaded the most ordinary acts of life. Here was that kind of courtesy and grace in the ordinary acts of life which had first attracted me in the life of St Francis of Assisi, and I soon found that it had its source in the Rule of St Benedict. "Let all guests who come," it was said, "be treated like Christ himself, for he will say, I was a stranger and you took me in." This was the sign for which I had been seeking. I saw now visibly present in the Church the spirit of Christ, which is the spirit of Charity, and I hesitated no longer.

I was received into the Church on Christmas Eve 1931 and made my first communion at the midnight mass in the little church at Winchcombe. It was a still moonlight night, and as I made my way past the great perpendicular parish church, where I had previously gone to communion, to the little Catholic church in a by-street, I knew that a new epoch had begun for me. I had found the hidden source of life which had once created the Cotswold world which I had loved and the civilisation of England, and which was now relegated to the by-streets of modern England. When I read the office of Matins for Christmas Day with its great

Sermon on the Incarnation by St Leo, I knew that I had found the authentic voice of Christianity, and that in the mass of that little church I was in communion with the Catholic Church throughout the world and throughout the ages.

It was less than a month after my reception into the Church that I entered the monastery to try my vocation as a monk. This was not done without considerable hesitation. I thought at first of becoming a Franciscan or a Dominican. I wanted above all to preach the truth which I had discovered, and it was only very slowly that it dawned on my mind that it was possible to follow Christ without becoming a preacher. I remember picking up a book in a bookshop in Cheltenham called *Christ the Ideal of the Monk* by Abbot Marmion, and wondering what the connection could be between the life of a monk and the life of Christ. In the course of time I was to read the book through again and again, until at last that ideal took complete possession of me.

I began to realise that it was possible to follow Christ without becoming a preacher. I saw that his preaching had occupied two or three years at most in the life of Christ and that it was not through that principally that his work had been accomplished. The greater part of his life had been spent in complete obscurity at Nazareth. I saw now that this hidden life, spent in a small village away from the world, among peasants and small craftsmen, was a model of the life of every Christian and was, moreover, the very thing to which I had felt myself drawn.

When I went on to read the history of monasticism in Montalembert's great work on the Monks of the West, I discovered that it was by men who followed the example of Christ in this way that the conversion of Europe had been achieved. St Benedict had lived at the critical moment in history when the Roman Empire had just collapsed. The death of the last Roman Emperor coincided with his birth. He found the world in ruins and set about rebuilding it not by preaching and teaching but by organising the monastic life. He drew men apart from the world and set them to a life of prayer and work.

It was in this way that our European civilisation had been built up in the Dark Ages. From the monastery with its daily round of agriculture and craftsmanship had grown up the villages and towns of medieval Europe. In the monastic library had been stored the books which remained from the old Classical culture to become the source of a new culture in the Middle Ages. But above all, by the prayer of the monks had been laid those deep foundations of spiritual life on which the whole life of Europe had been based. I saw now that Christianity was not just a doctrine to be preached but a life to be lived, and that the very heart of that life was to be found in sacrifice. It was not by his work or by his preaching but by the sacrifice of his life on the Cross that Christ had saved the world, and the monk was one who was called to offer his life in sacrifice day by day in his work and his prayer in union with Christ on the Cross.

This ideal of sacrifice, however, was to lead to the first great crisis of my monastic life. Though the life in the monastery was not an easy one, it was far less austere than that to which I had grown accustomed. The meals were simple but they were generous, and though there was no meat, there was an abundance not only of fruit and vegetables but also of cheese and eggs and fish and cereals. The beds were wooden with straw mattresses such as I was used to, and the cells were barely furnished with a desk and chair, but I had to get used to hot baths and central heating and other luxuries of that kind. It happened that soon after I entered the monastery the story of a Cistercian monastery was read in the refectory, as there was always reading during the meals. The Cistercian order was a reform of the Benedictine life which took place in the Middle Ages and introduced a far greater degree of austerity into the rule. As I listened it seemed to me that this was the ideal of life which I desired and I accordingly obtained permission to visit a Cistercian monastery on Caldey Island.

This was to give me one of the greatest lessons of my life. I had built up in my imagination an ideal, which had very little relation to reality, and as soon as I arrived I realised that I had made a mistake. The life had none of the attraction which I had expected. It was not that there was anything wrong with the life itself, but simply that I had been beguiled by my imagination. I realised then that what I had been seeking was a fantasy under which my own self-will was disguised. I realised then that the will of God was not to be found in following my own desires, however spiritual they might seem, but in seeking to adapt myself to those circumstances in which by divine providence I actually found myself. I had followed my own desires for so long and worked out my own ideal, that it was difficult for me to see that the process had now to be reversed. But I began to understand why St Benedict had turned away from the extreme austerities of the early monks of the Egyptian desert, and had made humility and obedience the basis of monastic life. I saw that the greatest obstacle in life was the power of self-will and that this could cloak itself in the desire to preach the Gospel or to live an austere life or in any other form of spiritual ambition. Once again it was the example of Christ which was the guiding principle, Christ who had said, "Learn of me for I am meek and humble of heart", and who had been made "obedient unto death".

This is, I suppose, the hardest lesson which it is possible for anyone who has been brought up in habits of independence to learn. Neither humility nor obedience had had any meaning for me, and it was characteristic that I had never even recognised them as virtues to be found in Christ. Now I began to see that the whole life of Christ could be regarded as one long act of obedience to the will of his Father. "My meat," he had said, "is to do the will of him who sent me", and the life of a Christian was simply the following of Christ in this obedience to the Father's will, that is to the order of divine providence.

There is a divine order in the universe, as I had long ago learned from Marcus Aurelius, and to discern the divine will beneath all the events of daily life and to adhere to it with one's own will was the source of all happiness. Human freedom can only be properly exercised in obedience to the divine law. The moment we set our own will in opposition to the order of the universe we make ourselves slaves to circumstances and lose our freedom of action. The only proper use of our freedom is freely to will what divine providence wills for us, to conform our wills by a free act of choice to the divine will.

But how is the divine will to be found? It can be found generally in the dictates of reason, but its perfect revelation is to be found in the law of the Church, for the Church exists to manifest the divine will to man. The monastic vow of obedience is therefore simply a means of bringing one's own will habitually into obedience to the will of God. I knew that in the mind of St Benedict the Abbot held the same place in the community as the bishop in the early Church; he was the representative of Christ. *Christi agere vices in monasterio creditur*, "he is believed to hold the place of Christ in the monastery", is St Benedict's phrase. To obey the Abbot therefore within the limits of the authority given him by the Rule was to obey Christ : "He who hears you, hears me", as Christ himself had said.

I found the path of obedience, though, made easier for me by the fact that I felt such a deep desire for community life. I had grown into such a state of isolation by following my own individual way, that I longed now to lose myself in the community. I saw in this the fulfilment of Christ's saying, "He who will lose his life for my sake will find it". The community represented Christ to me; it was a cell in his Mystical Body, that Body which extended throughout the world and was the living representative of Christ to all men. To love one's brethren was to love Christ; to serve one's brethren was to serve Christ. By devoting oneself to the community and learning to share more and more in the common life, one was sharing in the life of Christ, the life which he lives in his members on earth.

It was while I was learning this new conception of life that Hitler and Mussolini were rising to the height of their power in Europe, and I could not help seeing in this a challenge to our whole Western way of life. However grossly wrong their methods might be, they had understood like the Communists, the weakness of our Western individualism. Ever since the Renaissance Europe had concentrated its energies on the extension of material wealth and power and on the achievement of individual liberty. Now we were faced with the weakness of a civilisation in which the acquisition of wealth and the liberty of the individual were considered the supreme values in life. Both Fascism and Nazism and Communism in their different ways represented a challenge to this view of life by emphasising the value of sacrifice for the good of the community.

It was clear that both sides were wrong. The individual cannot be sacrificed to the community. The individual person is unique and inviolable and enjoys a right to freedom, which is subject only to the law of God. But the individual is not sufficient to himself, he needs the community in order to realise his personality. Man, as Aristotle had recognised, is a political animal; he is made for society. He is in a real sense a part of a whole, and he can only realise his true nature when he takes his place in the whole.

Yet he cannot sacrifice himself to a merely human society: that would be to surrender what is unique and most precious in him to a merely finite good, and could lead, as was only too clear, to the utter degradation of human nature. How to preserve his essential freedom and yet be able to find his place in a true social order, that was the dilemma. Our society had fought for freedom at all costs, and had split up its members into isolated atoms, which were in danger of losing all coherence. The Fascists and the Communists had sacrificed the freedom of the individual in order to organise the social order.

There is only one society in which the demands of liberty and authority, of the individual and society can be met. In the Christian community each individual can find his liberty in the total surrender of his life to God, because man is made for the absolute and nothing less can demand his entire obedience. At the same time he can give his life totally to the community, for the Christian community is the sole society in which the divine law is embodied, and to serve the community is to serve God. It is only when the good of the community is seen to be the participation of all its members in the life of Christ, which is the life of the Spirit, that the true ideal is to be found. Then the freedom of the individual is seen to consist in the free offering of himself to the community, in the free sacrifice of his life to Christ. Then the happiness of the individual is to be found in his exercising his allotted function in the community and acting as a member of the whole.

I saw then in the monastic community the pattern of the primitive Christian community. The early Church had been so filled with this sense of the community that it had practised strict Communism. "All things were held in common and no one presumed to call anything which he possessed his own . . . and distribution was made to each according as he had need". St Benedict had deliberately based himself on these words of the Acts of the Apostles and made the renunciation of all private property one of the essential marks of the monastic life. Each monk had to surrender everything which he possessed on entering the monastery, and when he made his final profession he renounced the power of private ownership altogether. Just as the monk's obedience was a free act of his own will made for the love of God in order to submit his will to the will of God, so his vow of poverty was a free act of renunciation

in order to surrender himself to the providence of God and
to make himself wholly dependent on the community. To
demand the surrender of a man's will or of his independence as the Fascists and Communists did, was to violate his
essential freedom and to make him a slave to the State.

While there was, therefore, perfect economic equality in
the monastery, each monk sharing equally in the goods of
the monastery and receiving all that he needed for his
personal use, there was also perfect social equality. St
Benedict had expressly stated that no distinction was to be
made between the son of a noble and the son of a serf, and
no class distinctions were recognised. One's position in the
community was determined by the time of one's entry,
apart from all considerations of age or experience. The
Abbot was elected freely by the monks from among themselves and he like all the rest was bound to obey the Rule.
All the more important matters concerning the community
were to be discussed in Chapter and in certain matters,
such as the election of new members, the vote of the community was decisive.

I myself was given a year's postulancy, or period of trial,
instead of the usual six months, as I had been received so
recently into the Church, before I was clothed as a novice.
During the noviciate which lasts one year, three "scrut-
inies" are held by the council of "deans" or senior monks
to decide whether the novice is fit to continue. At the end
of the year if he is considered suitable, he is put to the vote
of the Chapter, which consists of all the solemnly professed
monks of the community, and if he obtains a majority of
two-thirds of the votes, he is allowed to make his simple
profession. Simple profession consists of a vow to observe
poverty, chastity and obedience as a member of the community for the space of three years. At the end of three
years the monk is free to leave or the community may
decide to reject him, but if he again receives a two-thirds
majority of the Chapter vote, the Abbot may then decide
to allow him to make his solemn profession. Solemn pro-

fession according to the Rule of St Benedict consists of a vow of " stability, conversion of life and obedience ", which binds a monk to his community, like the vow of marriage, for life. I myself was clothed as a novice on 20th December 1933, being given the name of Bede, the Saint whose history had meant so much to me. I made my simple profession on 21st December 1934, and my solemn profession on 21st December 1937.

Each of these events was accompanied by most moving and impressive ceremonies, which revealed the true character of the act which one was performing. At the ceremony of clothing the whole community assembled in the Chapter-house and the Abbot washed the feet of the novice who was to be clothed, in imitation of Christ washing the feet of his disciples; and then each of the monks came up in turn and knelt down and kissed his feet. The novice was then clothed in the monastic habit and given a new name. Meanwhile the community sang the hymn : *Ubi caritas et amor, ibi deus est:*

Where there is love and charity, there is God.
The love of Christ has brought us together in unity,
Let us be glad and rejoice in him.

Nothing could make it clearer that it was Christ who was receiving you into the community and that it was in his person that you were being received. The clothing with the monastic habit itself was a sign that you were " putting on Christ ", and the new name signified that you had become a new man in Christ. The monastic habit is very simple. It consists of two garments, an under-garment, called the tunic, reaching down to the feet like the Greek tunic or *himation*; and a light garment with a hood attached thrown over it, like the Greek cloak or *chlamys,* and called a scapular. This has been the traditional clothing of man from time immemorial all over the world. It is common in one way or another to the Greek and the Roman, the Jew and the Arab, the Indian and the Chinese. Nothing could be more simple and dignified. But the monastic habit has not only a natural grace; it is also a symbol of a supernatural state. It shows the monk's status in society and marks him off as a man of prayer. It is a real loss to society when such diversities of costume go and the very idea of the life of prayer as having a function in society, as distinctive as that of a soldier or a sailor or a judge, is lost with it.

The ceremony of profession took place in the sanctuary of the church. The novice stood in the centre and read from a chart which he held in his hands a solemn promise to observe his vows. The chart was then placed·on the altar as a sign that the vows were offered to God. He then went down to the bottom of the church and with hands outstretched sang the verse of the Psalm :

Suscipe me, Domine, secundum eloquium tuum et vivam;
Et non confundas me ab expectatione mea.

Uphold me, O Lord, and I shall live;
And do not confound me in my expectation.

This was repeated three times as he advanced up the choir and into the sanctuary, and taken up each time by the choir in a chant of a most moving character. He was then clothed in the cowl, a heavy outer garment with long sleeves which is the choir dress of the monk, and went to kneel at the feet of the Abbot and each of the other professed monks in turn to receive the kiss of peace. He was now a member of the monastic family, sharing in all its goods and privileges, and committed to it for better or for worse until death. Finally the newly-professed monk lay down prostrate on the floor of the sanctuary for the rest of the mass.

This was the most symbolic gesture of all. He was offering himself as a living sacrifice to God in union with the sacrifice of Christ which was being enacted at the altar. From this time he had no power over himself either to possess anything or to do anything apart from the community to which he was joined. His life was entirely consecrated to God. This was the means by which he identified his life with the life of Christ, making an offering of himself to God in Christ.

The sacrifice was essentially a sacrifice of love. This is the very essence of monastic life. It is not simply a life of obedience under a rule; it is a life of love. It is the love of Christ which constrains a man to become a monk, and it is the love of his brethren in Christ which is the ruling principle of his life. We have almost lost this idea of Christian love. We tend to think of love as a passion which is based on sex and finds expression in family life. But there is a love of God which is no less a passion; which takes possession of the soul and demands its complete surrender, and which finds expression in another kind of family, the supernatural family, whose life is the life of grace. This is the real significance of the vow of chastity. It is not merely a negative renunciation of sex; it is the means of a positive fulfilment of one's whole being in the love of Christ.

The basis of all love is self-sacrifice. For love is the total giving of oneself to another. But it is impossible to give oneself totally to any other human being. It is the illusion of romanticism that the ideal of love can be realised in any human being. This is why all romantic love when it is realistic is tragic. It consists in seeking the satisfaction of an infinite desire in a finite and defective being. For human love is really infinite in its capacity. The tragedy of life arises from the fact that we all seek to satisfy this infinite desire with finite objects, with the beauty of nature or a human form. Plato in the Symposium had clearly shown how if our love is ever to be satisfied we must learn to ascend from the love of the human form to the love of human character and institutions, and finally through the love of Ideas to the love of Beauty itself, the absolute, infinite, unchanging beauty, which is also truth and goodness.

How can this ideal love be translated into human terms? That is the problem to which Plato gave no solution, but in Christianity this translation has been made. Christ is this absolute beauty manifested in a human form, in a human character. He is the one person whom it is possible to love to an infinite degree. The whole of Christianity really centres on this transformation of human love which is brought about by the love of Christ. In Christian marriage man and woman can really love one another with an infinite love, because each gives himself to Christ in the other. This is the total sacrifice of love for which our nature craves. Like everything in Christianity it is a sacramental love : it is a revelation of the Spirit in the flesh. In this relation sex becomes what it was always intended to be, a symbol or sacramental sign of love. The union of spirits is brought about by the union of flesh.

It is the tragedy of the modern world that the real significance of sex has been completely lost. In Hardy's *Jude the Obscure,* which reflects perhaps more than any other novel of its period the disillusionment of the modern spirit, the heroine, Sue Bridehead, is most indignant because she finds the Song of Songs in the Authorised Version of the Bible interpreted as referring to the love of Christ for the Church. But in reality it marks the profound insight of the Church that it was able to discover this meaning in it.

The Song of Songs is an oriental love poem of great beauty which expresses the drama of human love in the most realistic manner. But precisely because all human love is "typical" or symbolic of divine love, the Church was able to discover this deeper meaning in it. So it came about that from the earliest times the Song of Songs was interpreted in the Church as a symbol of the love of the soul for God, or rather of the love of the Word incarnate for human nature.

It is only when sex is understood in this light as a symbol and a preparation for the love of God that its true meaning can be seen. Because man is a spirit in a body of flesh, he has to learn to love through the flesh. But carnal love can never be anything more than a phase in human life and a preparation for love on a deeper level of being. In every marriage a time comes when the function of sex ceases to serve its immediate purpose and the marriage of souls which it is the secondary function of sex to develop must take its place. It is then only that love begins to reach its fulfilment. This is the love for which we were created and which alone survives in the Kingdom of Heaven, where we are told that there is neither marrying nor giving in marriage. It is a tragic illusion when the shadow or symbol is mistaken for the reality, and the reality is regarded as a fantasy and a substitute.

The object of the vow of chastity is simply to develop this power of love in the soul. By setting a man free from the ties of family life, it sets him free to love with a universal love. It is, of course, a special vocation, but it has its place not only in Christianity but in all the great religious traditions of mankind, and it has a firm psychological foundation. Every instinctive desire, it has been said, must be satisfied; what therefore cannot be satisfied in the flesh must be satisfied in the spirit. This transformation of love from sexual into spiritual love, from *eros* into *agape*, is indeed the very purpose of life. It is a long, difficult and painful process; it involves a kind of crucifixion of our nature. All our natural passions and affections have to be surrendered, not to be destroyed but to be transformed. We have to learn to be detached from every form of passion, if we are to become free to love without restraint. This means that we have to surrender ourselves without reserve to the love of God. The smallest degree of selfishness will spoil any love, and the love of God demands complete self-surrender. We have to give all that we may receive all.

This is the reason for all Christian asceticism. As long as we remain attached to anything, to bodily comfort or to friends, to any skill that we may have in art or science, above all, as long as we seek our own will in anything, we cannot receive the love of God into the depths of our being. But here is the paradox. As soon as we have renounced all these things for the love of God, we receive them back in a new way. We cannot love nature as it should be loved until we have renounced the love of nature. We cannot love our friends as they should be loved until we have renounced human affection. For it is only when we have renounced all selfish attachment to people and to things that we can love them purely for themselves in the love of God.

I do not pretend that I had worked all this out in the early stages of my life as a monk; on the contrary, it took years of painful experience. But I found gradually that I was being given back all that I had thought that I was giving up. I no longer pursued the beauty of nature as the object of my love and worship, but it entered now quite simply into my life as a permanent background within which I could live in harmony, and yet so transfigured by the presence of God that sometimes I felt like Adam in Paradise. Love for others which could never find an outlet before now began to fill my whole being, as I learned what it meant to love another person in Christ. It meant that behind each human soul with all its limitations and its failure to communicate itself, one could find the person of Christ, the power of an infinite love communicating itself to each and uniting each with the other and with all men.

It was not only that love was immeasurably enriched in height and in depth; I found that it was also extended in its range. Not long after I had been solemnly professed, I was made guestmaster of the monastery. St Benedict had said that guests would never be lacking in a monastery and with us there were always people staying in the monastery for one reason or another. At the week-ends there were often five or six at a time, and in the summer as many as twelve or fifteen. They came from all classes and professions and with all kinds of different religious backgrounds. I thus found myself with a continually expanding circle of friends, larger perhaps than I should ever have known if I had stayed in the world. At the same time I was able to meet them on the level not merely of social intercourse, but of the deeper needs of the spiritual life. Some came who were without any religion and were seeking for faith; others came because they had experienced difficulties in their faith or their allegiance. Some came simply for a rest from the turmoil of life, others came suffering from the effects of illness, a nervous breakdown or some other misfortune. In the course of time there were very few forms of human need which were not brought to our doors, and there were few who went away without receiving some help. Often I have known a man's life to be completely changed as the result of his stay in the monastery.

In all this there was but one means of help which we had to offer, the power of prayer. One could do what was possible by way of showing kindness and talking over difficulties, but ultimately it was prayer alone which prevailed. It is only in prayer that we can communicate with one another at the deepest level of our being. Behind all words and gestures, behind all thoughts and feelings, there is an inner centre of prayer where we can meet one another in the presence of God. It is this inner centre which is the real source of all life and activity and of all love. If we could learn to live from that centre we should be living from the heart of life and our whole being would be moved by love. Here alone can all the conflicts of this life be resolved and we can experience a love which is beyond time and change.

I felt something of this a little while after my solemn profession when my mother died. I went to see her when she lay unconscious in hospital, and though I was never able to speak to her again, I did not feel a sense of separation. We had been separated for many months at a time now, separated not only in space but also in thought. But as I knelt by her side I knew that I was united to her in the depths of my being, where neither time nor space nor change nor misunderstanding could have any place. For her to die was to pass through this world of shadows, beyond thought and feeling and sense, into that inner sanctuary of truth and love where one day we would be united for ever.

CHAPTER NINE

THE WORK OF GOD

When I was told that the monastic life was a "contemplative" life, I was at first at a loss to understand it. I think that my conception of contemplation was derived from the image of the Buddha seated cross-legged in perfect tranquillity, and there was nothing I saw in the monastery which seemed to have the least relation to this. On the contrary, there was an atmosphere of incessant activity. The whole day was taken up in a constant round of duties, in the choir, in the house, in the garden, in the workshops, which left very little leisure for "contemplation". It is true that there was a half-hour every day after vespers which was given to silent prayer, but it was difficult to see how this half-hour could be said to determine the character of the whole life.

It was some time before I learned the true nature of contemplation. Contemplation is a habit of mind which enables the soul to keep in a state of recollection in the presence of God whatever may be the work with which we are occupied. In this sense it is the true aim of every Christian life. But it is obvious that it is impossible to do this without some definite training. The monastic life is simply an organisation of life for this specific end. It has been worked out in the course of many centuries and goes back in fact to apostolic times, but its basic structure is very simple.

The whole day is divided into periods of three hours, and at the beginning of each period an "office" or service of prayer takes place by which that period of the day is consecrated to the service of God. The day, according to the Roman reckoning on which it is based, begins at six

148

o'clock and at this hour the office of *Prime* is said. *Terce* (Latin "*tertia hora*") follows at nine, *Sext* (Latin "*sexta hora*") at noon, *None* (Latin "*nona hora*") at about three in the afternoon, *Vespers* (Latin, *vespertina hora*") or Evensong) at six, and finally *Compline* (Latin "*Completorium*", the hour which "completes" the day) at about nine in the evening.

In addition to all these offices during the day, there is also the night-office or Vigil, which is generally said between four and five o'clock in the morning. This office is the oldest of all and forms the basis of the whole. The early Christians used always to meet for the Eucharist or Breaking of Bread in the evening, and the custom grew up of holding a meeting for prayers before it, which was known as the Vigil. This came eventually to be delayed till after midnight and the Eucharist was celebrated in the early hours of the morning. This Vigil was constructed on the same lines as the Jewish service in the synagogue, and consisted of readings from the Scriptures, and later from the Fathers of the Church, interspersed with Psalms.

This is the basis on which all the "hours" of the day are constructed. The Psalms form the principal element in the whole service by night and day, and the whole of the Psalter is used in the normal course of the week. This is the method of prayer which gradually took shape in the early Church and was completed by St Benedict. It takes up several hours of the day and forms a kind of framework into which all the work and other occupations of the day have to be fitted. From the first hour of the day to the last hour at night there is a continual movement from the choir to work or study or meals or recreation, and back again to choir. It sets up a kind of rhythm or pattern by which all the different actions of the day are related to one another, and to their source in God.

For us the day began at four o'clock when we all assembled in the church for Matins. The church had been originally the private chapel of the house and still retained some of the fifteenth-century stained glass. It was a long low room with a small sanctuary which had been built on in the early years of the present century. It was a pleasant homely place without any pretensions and exactly corresponded with what St Benedict in his Rule had called the "oratory of the monastery", a room in the house set apart for prayer. From the windows one looked out over the fields to the plain of Gloucester and the Malvern hills, and often when we assembled for Matins in the summer the song of the birds would come pouring in through the window, and I felt that we were joining our voices with the choir of nature in praise of the Creator. Matins and Lauds which followed it lasted normally a little over an hour, but on Sundays and feast days it took nearly two hours. Yet the lessons and the psalmody and the chant were so varied that it never palled, and even now after twenty years it still retains for me all its original charm and freshness. After Lauds we returned to our cells for what St Benedict calls "the necessities of nature", that is to wash and shave and make beds and clean out the cells, and we then assembled at six o'clock for Prime. Prime took only half-an-hour and was followed by the mass at which all those who were not priests made their communion. After mass came Pittance. St Benedict allowed for only two meals during the day, as was customary at that time, dinner and supper. In modern times a breakfast, called "pittance", has been added, which with us consisted of tea or coffee and bread or toast and butter, and was taken standing up in our places in the refectory. There was an interval for reading after pittance and then we assembled for the short office of Terce and the High Mass at eight-thirty.

The day's work began at about nine-thirty. The morning was usually given to study and the afternoon to manual work of different kinds. Dinner was at midday. All the meals were taken in the refectory in silence, and at dinner and supper there was reading from a book at a lectern. We all took our turns at reading and in the course of the year a great many books were read in this way. At dinner the reading was usually history or biography or travel or something of general interest; at supper it was usually a life of a saint or something of a religious nature. During the war we always had the important news read from *The Times,* and on Sunday something from the *Tablet* or one of the other weekly papers. The meal always began and ended with grace which was solemnly chanted and concluded after dinner in the church. In this way the meals in the refectory were kept in relation with the divine office in choir, and had something of a sacred character.

It was, in fact, the governing principle of the life that nothing was profane. One was serving God just as much when taking a meal or working or studying as when chanting the office in choir. This was emphasised by the fact that those who were serving or reading in the refectory each received a special blessing at the beginning of the week, in which they were to enter on their duties. After dinner we were allowed a rest of an hour, called meridian, when one could either read or sleep, and after the afternoon work we had a bowl of tea in the refectory, called *caritas,* which was taken like pittance standing in silence. Vespers was at five-fifteen followed by a half-hour of silent prayer, then supper and afterwards recreation. This was the only time during the day when talking was freely allowed, but on Sundays and feast days there were longer recreations and walks outside. The day closed with Compline, which was always sung in the dark with just two candles burning on either side of the altar. At the end of the office these were extinguished and the prayers were concluded in the dark. After Compline complete silence was observed until after Prime the next day.

Each day from before dawn till after dark was thus set within a round of prayer which determined the character of the whole life. In this way the whole day was given a sacred character, which influenced every activity. This is something which has been completely lost in the modern world, but which is found among almost all primitive peoples. We know that in the primitive tribal community the pattern of life was determined by the ceremonial rites and dances which embodied the ancient traditions of the tribe. In this tradition the whole of life was seen as a sacramental mystery. The divine presence was believed to make itself known under all the varying forms of nature and in all circumstances of human life.

In this vision of life there is nothing which is not holy. The simplest actions of eating and drinking, of washing and cleaning, of walking and sitting, of lying down and rising from rest, have a sacramental character; they signify something beyond themselves and are intimately related to religious rites. So also every form of work, especially everything connected with the round of agriculture, of ploughing and harrowing, sowing and reaping, milking and tending the cows and sheep, is part of a sacramental mystery, by which we enter into communion with the rhythm of nature and take part in that ritual by which the life of man is continually renewed. The craft of the carpenter, the ironworker, the potter and the weaver is likewise a " mystery ", not merely a practical concern but a means of initiation into the mysterious laws of nature and of co-operation in her creative activity. There is no reason, of course, why the mechanic and the electrician should not be a craftsman in this sense. Their craft is concerned with the more subtle and hidden laws of nature, but it is no less strictly dependent on the law of God.

Now it was through the monastic life that the dignity of labour was restored to Europe. In the Roman Empire, which bears so close a resemblance in so many ways to our own civilisation, the significance of manual labour had been lost through the introduction of slavery, just as it has been lost in the modern world through industrialism. But the monastic life restored it to its proper place in human life.

Who sweeps a room as for thy laws
Makes that and the action fine,

George Herbert wrote, and this is the principle which governs all monastic work. By the vow of obedience every action of the day is consecrated to God and is therefore given a sacred character.

During my early years in the monastery there were very few kinds of work which I was not called on to do. We took our turns in serving meals in the refectory and in washing up. Then there was all the housework to be done, including scrubbing the floors. But on most days there would be a period of work outside in the garden or on the farm or in one of the workshops. During the hay and corn harvest most of the community would turn out and we would often work on late into the evening. In the same way, for the planting and lifting of the potatoes twenty or more monks would be sent out to work on through the morning and afternoon. We wore hooded blue cotton smocks for work and this often made the work a picturesque sight, when twenty or thirty figures would be seen moving up and down the field. Thus the rhythm of the seasons formed a constant background to our life and for the first time in my life I felt that I was living in harmony with the course of nature. I found also that I learned to look on nature with new eyes. I was no longer a spectator merely, but taking my part in the universal plan, and I felt myself to be an element in an ordered scheme of existence.

At other times I was occupied in the laundry or in the carpenter's shop or helping the electrician in the engineering shop, but most commonly I was employed on building. There was always some work of repair or of new building going on, and I took a hand in plastering and building of all kinds and especially in mixing concrete. At first we did all the work by hand, but later we had a concrete mixer which enabled us to build a whole new block of farm buildings. In work of this kind we usually had a foreman from outside working over us, and the brothers learned their trade from him. In this way some became skilled brick-layers and gradually mastered the whole art of building. In the same way, others learned weaving and pottery and we made the stuff for our habits and vestments, and eventually developed a large pottery. Those who like myself had no particular skill were called on to assist in the unskilled work wherever it might be needed.

In this way one became familiar with work of all kinds and one's life fitted into a pattern of regular work. I dis-covered also something of the fraternity which is formed among those who work together over a long period of time and I learned the respect which is due to the good work-man. The work often brought us into contact with work-men from outside, lorry-drivers, quarrymen and labourers, and I discovered how much natural pride every workman has in his job. Outside work, however, is not seen in any relation to religion; it has no place in a universal plan. The labourer feels himself to be the slave of a system for which he has no respect. It is only when the work is done for God, as part of man's co-operation in the divine plan, that its hardships and inevitable conflicts and frustrations can be endured, and the workman can feel himself to be sharing in the labour and the suffering of Christ.

I found now that the problem of machinery no longer presented itself to me in the same light. The problem re-mained, but it was no longer the insuperable obstacle which it had been. I saw now that any work which was done in obedience to the will of God, however dull and mechanical it might be, could be made a genuine " sacri-fice ", an offering to God. The very misery and sense of frustration which went with it could be turned to account. It could become a means of suffering with Christ, of offer-ing one's life to God on behalf of one's fellow men. At the same time I saw that there was no reason why machinery should not be so used that it not only relieves human drudgery but can also be made the instrument for producing better work. There is beauty in the products of the machine, in a car, a ship, an aeroplane, when it is used according to the true purposes of nature. The evil of industrialism has been due to the abuse of the machine, to the lust for material wealth and the contempt for the rights of the human person. If the machine were used in the service of God and with respect to the fundamental needs of human nature, then it could take its place in a true human society.

But the problem remains. So often the machine seems to be of value only in producing things more quickly or more easily or in greater quantity, and not in making them intrinsically better and therefore more beautiful. Then again it is rarely that a machine gives the human workman real satisfaction. It does not call forth his powers in the same way as the work of the hands. It may demand more skill and ingenuity in some ways, but it does not touch his feelings and his sensibility, his heart and imagination. The craftsman can put his whole soul into his work; it can become the means for the fulfilment of his being. So it appears that there is still a place for craftsmanship in human life. The machine may be indispensable in a society organised on a world-wide scale as at the present day, but if a society is to be really human, there will always be a need for the hand-craftsman.

In a monastic community this was especially evident, because tending a machine could never give the same scope to prayer as working with the hands. It set up a different rhythm and to some extent made the worker subordinate to the machine. But in working with one's hands, whether it was in field or farm work, in making pots on the wheel or weaving on the loom, one could put one's prayer into one's work, and make an offering of mind and heart and hand to God. This was surely the principle which underlay the beauty of the work of the medieval craftsman, and of almost all primitive art. He was in contact with that mystery of Being which underlies all outward forms,

and so caught a reflection of the eternal beauty in his art.
This can be felt especially when the work of the hands is
actually made for use in the divine service. One can see it
in all the early religious art of India and China, no less
than of Egypt and Greece, and of Christian Europe. There
is a quality in the art of the Ajanta frescoes and the painting of the Tang dynasty in China, in early Egyptian and
Greek sculpture, with which no later art can compare. In
the same way the greatest period of Christian art was in the
early centuries, from the fifth to the twelfth century. This
was the period of the great development of Plain Chant, of
the art of Mosaic, of the Greek icon and the Romanesque
basilica. In this art the Christian genius found its authentic
expression because it was an art which was wholly directed
towards divine worship.

The centre of Christian worship was the altar, the place
of sacrifice, and it was round this that the church was built.
The mosaics with which it was decorated were not mere
decorations; they were sacred images, by means of which
the mind was to be raised to the contemplation of the
divine mysteries, just as the chant was not merely an
accompaniment to the words of the Psalms and antiphons,
but an integral element in the prayer.

This is the tradition which is inherited in the Benedictine
monastery. These centuries, from the fifth to the twelfth,
are what Newman called the Benedictine centuries. They
correspond with what are called the "dark ages", and
there is something very significant in this. It was an age of
very little culture and of the most elementary civilisation;
it might be called a "night of the spirit". But it was precisely in this night of the spirit that the seeds of all our
European culture were sown. Human life needs its periods
of darkness as well as of light. The seed has to be sown in
the darkness of the earth in the winter, in order that it
may come to birth in the spring. It was in this night of the
"dark ages" that Europe learned the secret of contemplation.

When material civilisation had collapsed and the light of culture was almost extinguished, then it was that men turned to that mystery of truth which lies beyond the material world and beyond all human wisdom. They had little human learning. They had the Bible, they had the commentaries of the Fathers of the Church, and they had some remains of classical learning, which were preserved in the monasteries. It was from these sources that their contemplation was fed : it was from them that the great structure of the sacred liturgy was built up. We have grown so accustomed to the idea that the material world and human history are the proper object of human study that we find it difficult to understand a world in which these studies played so little part. To the medieval man the supreme event in human history, which transcended all the wonders of the material world, was the incarnation of the Son of God.

This is the perspective which we have to recover if we are to understand the secret of monastic life. No matter how vast the space of the stellar universe may be, or how extensive the span of time which we must allow for the evolution of the world, neither space nor time are of any significance in comparison with the fact that at a certain point in space and time the eternal, infinite Being, which we call God, was manifested in the span of a human life. This is the supreme fact in comparison with which all human science and history pales into insignificance.

This was the object of human contemplation in the Middle Ages; this was the inspiration which built up the great monastic and cathedral churches. Just as behind all the great civilisations of the past, of Egypt and Babylon, of China and India, of Mexico and Peru, there lies the inspiration of a religion, which contemplated the divine mystery which is manifested in the regular course of nature and of human life; so behind the medieval civilisation lies the religion which contemplated the greater mystery of the manifestation of the divine nature in the human nature of Christ. But this was never a merely theoretical contemplation. Just as the pagan who contemplated the course of nature, the movement of the stars, the dying of the vegetation in the winter and its rising again in the spring, strove to participate in the divine mystery and to share in the divine life; so the Christian who contemplates the life of Christ, desires to share in that life, to die with him and to rise again to a new and immortal life. This is the mystery which underlies the sacred liturgy. It is a means by which the Christian may share in the life and death and resurrection of Christ. The music of the chant, the ceremonial of the choir, the use of candles and incense, are all so many signs by which the sacred drama may be impressed on the soul and become part of its own inner life.

It is here that the true function of art becomes apparent. Art like everything else in modern life has become separated from religion; but in the beginning, it was not so. The function of art, from the earliest times of which we have any knowledge in the palaeolithic caves, has been to invoke the divine presence. Man can only approach the divine mystery by means of images, and it is the work of the artist to represent or "make present" the divine mystery in an image in such a way that the people may enter into communion with it. This is why art in early times is so closely associated with magic, because the image is held to be charged with the divine power. So also in early Christian art, particularly in the mosaic art of the early centuries as it can be seen at Ravenna or in some of the early churches in Rome, the aim of the artist was to depict the mystery of the faith in symbolic terms, so that the minds of the worshippers might be raised to the contemplation of the divine mystery.

The perfection of this kind of art is to be found in plainchant, for the music of the chant has no other purpose than to raise the heart and mind to God in prayer. It is probably derived from the music of the Hebrew temple, and has certain affinities with Greek music, but its character is unique. It grew up in the early centuries with the divine office itself. Its basis was of extreme simplicity, just a variation on two or three notes in the singing of a Psalm or the recitation of a prayer; but gradually it acquired an extraordinary beauty, based not on the modern scale but on the Greek modes. It is strange at first to modern ears, but as its significance is grasped, it has an incomparable power over the soul, as Simone Weil has testified in recent times. It is a supernatural music, nearer to that of Bach and Palestrina than to any later style, but in its own way unexcelled.

It is this which gives such a strange and exalted power to the sacred liturgy. I had discovered long ago that in the Bible the Christian revelation was given in poetic terms which made the same kind of appeal as all great art. But now I found something more; the language of the Bible, of the old Latin Vulgate, was taken and woven into a kind of poetic drama and set to music. The whole Bible was seen as a single whole, a revelation of the Word of God, in which the Old Testament was interpreted in the light of the New. From Advent to Pentecost the mystery of the life of Christ was unfolded in all its stages; and from Pentecost onwards the mystery of the Church and her saints culminating in the feast of All Saints.

To take part in the liturgy was not merely to be a spectator of this drama. It was to share mystically in the life and death and resurrection of Christ, to receive the gift of the Spirit at Pentecost and to participate in the communion of the saints. Here all the arts were combined in the exercise of their highest function. The architecture of the church, the sculpture and painting on the walls, the music of the chant and the colour and shape of the vestments and the hangings on the altar, the ceremonies of the choir and sanctuary, as solemn and rhythmic as a ritual dance, were all used to show forth the mystery of the divine Word; to manifest it not in abstract terms to the reason only, but in its concrete embodiment, appealing to eye and ear, to sense and imagination, to heart and soul. Yet all this outward splendour was strictly subordinated to its end, to enable the soul to pass through the outward form to its inner meaning, to contemplate the Word of God, to be moved by the action of the Holy Spirit. This was what gave to it all a timeless character. It was the representation of the mystery of the Eternal manifested in time, the Light coming out of darkness, the Word being born out of the Silence, God becoming man.

But the centre of the whole of this mystery, of course, was to be found in the daily sacrifice of the mass. Every day each priest said his mass in the early hours of the morning, and every day the whole community of choir monks assembled for the solemn High Mass after Terce. This was the real pivot of the monastic day. It had all the solemnity of vestments with their different colours for the different seasons of the year, marking symbolically the stages in the drama of the Christian mystery. There were the candles burning on the altar and the incense going up in smoke in token of the prayer and sacrifice which ascend to heaven. And at the centre of it all there was the mystery of the Bread and the Wine. Here were the fruits of the earth, the tokens of man's labour, which have been offered in sacrifice from the beginning of history, and were prefigured in the offering of Melchisedec in the Old Testament. Here the offering was made of all the work of men's hands, of all our own work in the service of God, of all the toil of those who labour throughout the world. The gifts were placed on the altar, and the words of consecration were said over them : " This is my Body, this is my Blood."

In an instant everything was changed. Our gifts had been taken into the hands of Christ; they had been blessed and consecrated, and now they had been transformed into him. The earthly elements had been transfigured, and by this transfiguration all human labour had been given a new meaning. By being offered to God under the signs of the bread and the wine, it had been taken up into the sacrifice of Christ. It had been sanctified by him and made part of his own sacrifice for the salvation of the world. By this all human labour had been made sacred, because it had been brought into relation with the labour of Christ for man's salvation.

But in all this one was not merely a spectator. Whether one's place was in the choir or in the sanctuary, one took one's part in the offering which was being made by the whole community. The Body of Christ was assembled to make the offering of itself through its Head to God. The priest was the representative of Christ and made the offering in his name, but the deacon and the subdeacon had each their function to perform. Then there were the acolytes who assisted the ministers and carried candles and incense, and the choir with its scholar to lead the chant. Every member had his part to play, not only by singing but by sharing in the ceremonies, both of choir and sanctuary. There were times for the choir to stand with heads uncovered, to bow down or kneel in prayer, to sit with the hood raised to cover the head for the reading of the Epistle, to stand again for the Gospel, or to recline for the chanting of Gloria and Creed.

All these ceremonies were part of an elaborate ritual which was intimately related to the action which was taking place in the sanctuary. For we were taking part in an action. All the chanting and the ceremonial were but details in one great ritual action by which the sacrifice of Christ was to be enacted among us. For this is the real meaning of the mass. It is a ritual action by which the sacrifice of Christ is made present to us by means of outward signs and we are enabled to participate in it. Once again it is the mystery of the eternal order manifested in time. The sacrifice of Christ belongs to the eternal order. He, the eternal Word of God, assumed our human nature; he united it in one person with himself. He offered this human nature as a sacrifice once in history on the Cross, and raised it up to eternal life in himself. But he left his disciples under the signs of Bread and Wine the means by whicl that eternal sacrifice could be made present in time, and they by sharing in his sacrifice could share in his eternal life.

We were gathered, then, to take our part not merely in the chant and the ceremonies but in the sacrifice of Christ himself. We were offering ourselves, our souls and bodies, through the words and actions of the mass, as a sacrifice to God. And God accepted our sacrifice. At the moment of consecration, as our gifts of bread and wine were transformed into the body and the blood of Christ, so we ourselves were transformed into him. He was present among his disciples, making himself known to them, as of old, in the breaking of bread. Time and space were obliterated, and we were gathered into that eternal present, in which all things stand in their essential unity before God. This was the centre around which not only our own life but the life of the whole world moved. All the movements of the stars and the atoms, the course of biological evolution and of human history, all derived their meaning from this. For Christ is the Head not only of all mankind but of the whole physical universe; all things, in St Paul's words, are to be gathered to a head in him. When he assumed a human nature, he assumed the whole universe in a certain sense into himself. For by the incarnation the whole universe is brought into organic relation with Christ and raised to a new mode of existence in him. When we assisted at mass we were assisting at the mystery of the "new creation", by which the whole world is destined to be transformed, passing from its present mode of extension in time and space into the eternal order of being in God. The creation was revealed for what it is, a symbol of the eternal reality manifested in time, a process of "becoming" always moving towards its realisation in the order of absolute being, where each creature will participate according to its capacity in the divine glory.

But still more intimately we were assisting at the return of mankind to its lost unity. Through the sacrifice of

Christ mankind, which had been divided by sin, was restored to unity, and the sacrifice of the mass was the means by which this unity was being achieved. Sin operates constantly as a force by which mankind is being divided, husband against wife, parents against children, class against class, and nation against nation. The sacrifice of Christ was the supreme power acting against this power of sin and drawing men into the unity of his Church.

Every day before Compline we assembled in the Chapterhouse for a short period of reading from some spiritual book, and the names of all those who had asked for our prayers were read out. These requests came from all parts of the world and from people in all kinds of circumstances. Our prayers were asked for the sick and the suffering, for the dying and the dead; for those in spiritual and in material need; for those in prison and condemned to death. Then there were the more general needs of Church and State, and as the years moved on towards the world war and the sum of human misery increased, the need for prayer became ever more urgent. There were the Jews and Christians suffering persecution in Germany; the victims of the war in Spain, in Finland and in Greece; there was the martyrdom of Poland.

Then when the whole world became engulfed in war, it became clear that it was for the world that one must pray, for mankind sinning, suffering and dying in circumstances which recalled the world to which the Hebrew prophets had spoken and seemed to herald the fulfilment of the Apocalypse of St John. In all this there was but one thing which could give any meaning to life, and that was the Crucifixion. The mass of human suffering would remain utterly unintelligible, if we did not know that the one point in history, where the power of evil attained its greatest strength and human suffering was most acute, was also the point at which the love of God was most purely revealed.

Because God had suffered in our human nature and redeemed our nature by that suffering, therefore the suffer-

ing of every human being had been given an infinite and
eternal value. Each one suffered now not as an isolated
individual apart from his fellow men, but as the member of
a Body. It was Christ who suffered in each member of his
Body and made that suffering the means of its redemption.
Thus at the mass each day, where the mystery of redemption was made present sacramentally, one could offer the
suffering of all men to God, so that it might be taken up
into his redeeming act. For it is only in the eternal order,
where Christ is revealed as the Head of all mankind, suffering for all, dying for all, and rising again from the dead that
all may share a new life in him, that the mystery of evil
and suffering in this world can receive any meaning.

CHAPTER TEN

CATHOLICISM

Owing to the fact that I entered the monastery only a few weeks after my reception into the Church, my knowledge of Catholicism came to me almost entirely from the monastic community to which I now belonged. The monastic community represented the Church for me, and my knowledge of the faith came to me principally through my participation in the sacred liturgy. I felt therefore no break in my life such as I might have experienced if I had been thrown upon a parish. I entered a community which fulfilled all the desires of my life and I took part in a service of divine worship which transcended anything I had ever imagined in its beauty and significance.

But there were also periods which were given to study. In the Rule of St Benedict the day is divided between the Divine Office and prayer, which takes up about five hours of the day, and manual work, to which we usually gave up the afternoon, and finally what St Benedict calls "*lectio divina*", or sacred reading, to which we gave the hours which were free in the morning., This was the period which the monks of old gave to their study of the Bible and the Fathers of the Church, and this remained the basis of our own studies.

I found that I now had time to study the Old and the New Testaments in the light of modern research, no longer depending simply on my own insight. I came up also against the problem of the authority of the Church. I had to come to believe the Gospel by the effort of my own mind with scarcely any assistance from others, and I did not find it at all easy at first to submit my mind to the guidance of others. Nothing seemed further from my own experience

165

than the saying of St Augustine, "I would not believe the
Gospel, were it not for the authority of the Church." On
the contrary, I felt that it was only because I believed the
Gospel that I had come to accept the authority of the
Church. But I soon began to realise that however certain
I might be about the truth of the Gospel, my faith could
not rest on my own individual experience alone. It required to be supported by the witness of the universal
Church, and it was only when I accepted the authority of
the universal Church that my faith attained to complete
security.

So I began to learn the meaning of St Anselm's saying,
"*Credo ut intelligam*", "I believe in order that I may
understand". I found that when I submitted my mind to
the teaching of the Church, because I knew that teaching to
be inspired by God, my mind was given light to understand
what I believed and to enter more and more completely
into the mystery of Grace. I discovered that the faith contained mysteries infinitely beyond anything which I had
conceived, and that only in submitting my mind to the
teaching of the Church could I transcend my own limitations and enter into the full inheritance of the Catholic
faith.

However I did not find that in this way I was required
to accept anything which was contrary to my reason.

When I began the critical study of the New Testament I
found that the standard of historical criticism was far
beyond anything for which I had been prepared. The great
crisis in the historical study of the Gospels had occurred at
the beginning of this century with the movement known as
Modernism in the Catholic church. The leaders of this
school tried to make a distinction between the "Jesus of
history", and the "Christ of theology". They denied the
historical character of the Gospels, but maintained that it
was still possible to believe in Christ as the Word of God.
This was perhaps the most destructive heresy since the
great heresies of the fourth and fifth centuries, which had

denied the union of the two natures, of man and God, in Christ. It was naturally condemned by the Church, but it had the effect of bringing to birth a school of historical criticism, which proceeded to establish the truth of the Gospel narratives in the light of modern scholarship with greater exactitude than ever before. The work of the great French scholars of the early years of this century, Lagrange, Lebreton, Prat and De Grandmaison, has in fact placed the evidence of the Gospels on a historical basis which is perfectly secure, though unhappily the destructive criticism of an earlier period still creates a prejudice in many people's minds.

When I went on to study Church history and the Fathers, I found the same exact scholarship applied to the evidence for the growth and development of the Church. I was able to study at length all the texts which Newman had adduced to show the historical continuity of the Papacy, and what I had seen before intuitively in a general view, I could now grasp in all its detail. Thus at each step reason and faith went together. This is not to say that there were not often conflicts and difficulties. Apart from the doctrinal decisions of the Church, there is a vast field of study and speculation where there are conflicting and diverse views.

As time went on I found that there was immense scope for the exercise of one's critical faculties, and that the use of reason was not impeded but rather stimulated by the constant effort to keep it in vital relation to the truth of faith. Faith and reason could not conflict in reality; where there was an apparent conflict, it gave a certain zest to one's study to try to resolve it without prejudice to the one or to the other.

My Master of Studies at that time was an old Keble scholar, who had a good knowledge of Hebrew as well as of Latin and Greek, and a mind of an encyclopædic character. He always maintained that a monk should strive to know "something of everything and everything of something", and encouraged me to read as widely as possible.

As soon as I had made my simple vows I began the study of philosophy in preparation for the priesthood, and after my solemn vows I began theology. I was finally ordained a priest on 9th March 1940.

The basis of all these studies was the *Summa Theologica* of St Thomas, which I had already begun to study before. This is the most perfect synthesis of Christian doctrine which has ever been made.. The science of theology was built up during the first centuries of the history of the Church by the great Fathers of the Greek and Latin Church. Their method was to apply to the doctrine of the Christian faith, contained in the sacred scriptures and in the tradition of the Church, the exact methods and language of Greek philosophy. The early Fathers were mostly Platonists, and Christian doctrine received in their hands a predominantly Platonic character, which was most evident in the work of St Augustine in the West. During the Dark Ages little advance was made, but in the eleventh century with St Anselm a new development began, and this came to a head in the thirteenth century, with the discovery of the works of Aristotle, in the theology of St Thomas Aquinas.

St Thomas was a philosopher in his own right of the same stature as Plato or Aristotle, and he brought to the study of Christian doctrine the most exact and comprehensive, lucid and penetrating mind which has ever been known.

At the same time he was a man of deep faith and the inheritor of a continuous tradition of Christian life and thought, so that his work may be said to mark the culmination of the Christian genius. In it faith and reason found their most perfect balance and the consistency of Christianity with all that is best in human thought was demonstrated as it had never been done before.

I think that the book which made me realise the full extent of St Thomas's achievement was Etienne Gilson's *Spirit of Medieval Philosophy*. This is the work of one who is himself a master both of ancient and of modern philosophy, and places the whole tradition of Christian philosophy from St Augustine to St Thomas in its true setting as one of the great cultural movements of history. And yet it is not long ago that the history of philosophy was supposed to have ended with the last of the Greek philosophers and only to have begun again with Descartes.

Not less instructive than Gilson's work was Maritain's *Degrees of Knowledge,* in which an attempt is made to bring St Thomas's philosophy in relation to modern science. St Thomas took his physical theories from Aristotle, and it was the overthrow of Aristotle's *Physics,* which was responsible as much as anything for the eclipse of St Thomas and the whole medieval tradition. But Maritain was able to show that the basic principles of St Thomas's philosophy can be validly applied to modern physical theories, so as to form a harmonious system. Though there is much which remains to be done in this sphere there does not seem to be any reason to doubt that this is so.

At the same time Maritain was able to show the relation which properly exists between science, philosophy and theology in the general scheme of human knowledge. The disaster which has come upon modern thought is due to the attempt of science to assume the functions of philosophy and theology as a standard of thought, and order can only be restored when science learns once more to accept its limitations.

Perhaps the book which most helped me to see the possibilities of a synthesis of modern science and philosophy with the traditional Christian philosophy was E. I. Watkin's *Philosophy of Form,* a work of original insight and comprehensive vision, which deserves to be better known.

In the wider sphere of the relation of Christian thought and culture to other forms of culture and civilisation my guide was Christopher Dawson. I found in him a mind as wide in its range as that of Spengler, who had first attracted me to the study of history or as that of Arnold Toynbee, who has since made himself a master in this field. Christopher Dawson accepted Spengler's theory of the "Cycles of Civilisation", but he subjected it to a radical criticism. Civilisations had their rise and fall, but they were not determined, as Spengler had maintained, by the inevitable laws of history, nor, according to the Marxist view, by economic conditions. He allowed both for the play of economic forces and the interplay of social factors, but he found the basis of all culture and civilisation in the power of religion. In his *Age of the Gods* he showed how religion underlay the pattern of culture not only among all primitive peoples but also in the great civilisations of Egypt and Babylonia, and in the earliest known cultures all over the world. In his *Making of Europe* he showed how our European civilisation from the first to the tenth century had been built on the foundations of the Christian faith; and finally in his *Progress and Religion* he showed how the idea of Progress in the eighteenth and nineteenth centuries had come to falsify our view of history and to substitute the idea of secular progress for religion as the guiding principle of human society.

I saw now clearly the cause of that degradation of our civilisation which had disturbed me at Oxford, and I could see now that its root lay, as in the decay of all civilisations of the past, in the loss of religion as the basis of our culture and the substitution of material power and wealth. At the same time I began to see more and more clearly in Catholicism the source of a new Christian culture which would be able to make use of all the advances in modern science and history, and build up a new Christian civilisation.

It was partly through the influence of Christopher Dawson and partly through contact with several friends who shared my interest, that I later took up again the study of oriental thought. I realised that a Christian civilisation could no longer be of a merely European character. Not only was the Church now extended throughout the world, but we were becoming more and more aware of the importance of Asia and Africa both as political and cultural powers. I had, as I have said, read some of the classics of Eastern thought long ago, but I now began to study the history of Chinese and Indian philosophy systematically, and to obtain all the texts which I was able to do in English translations. From this reading I discovered that Indian philosophy could boast of a tradition going back as far as the beginnings of Greek philosophy in the sixth century B.C., and continuing to develop without a break, parallel with our Christian philosophy, through the Middle Ages and down to the present day.

Here was a great religious tradition comparable in extent and grandeur with our European tradition, showing an original power of thought as remarkable as that of the Greeks and yet completely different in its orientation. Whereas for the Greek man was the centre of the universe and everything was considered in relation to him, for the Indian the supreme reality was Brahma, the absolute Being, and the whole finite world of man and nature was regarded always in its relation to this absolute reality. Whether one considers the Hindu or the Buddhist tradition, the effort of thought which has gone to the making of this philosophy is immense and constitutes one of the greatest achievements of human culture. The weakness of Indian thought is, no doubt, that in its preoccupation with the one supreme reality it has tended to deny the reality of the finite world, but it would seem that this is precisely the corrective which is needed for our modern science which has come to regard the material world as the unique reality.

Certainly from a Christian point of view the importance of Indian philosophy can hardly be over-estimated. It marks the supreme achievement of the human mind in the natural order in its quest of a true conception of God.

The idea of God which is found in Sankara, the great doctor of the Vedanta, is almost identical with that of St Thomas. According to him God is *sacchidananda,* that is, absolute Being (*sat*), absolute Knowledge (*chit*), and abso-lute bliss (*ananda*). He is eternal, infinite, unchanging, incomprehensible, the One "without a second ". In Him (or It, for the divine Being is as much beyond personality in any human sense as it is beyond all else that we can conceive), exists every kind of perfection which we can conceive in a manner which transcends all thought and all expression. Before this inexpressible mystery we can only say, "*Neti, Neti* ", "Not this, Not that ". And yet, and this is the very starting point of all Indian thought, this absolute, incomprehensible mystery of Brahma is one with the mystery which lies at the heart of our human life. Brahma is the Atma, He is the true Self of every man; each of us can find his true being only in God.

And so the whole movement of Hindu philosophy culminates in the practice of Yoga, the search for "union" with God. It is not like Greek philosophy primarily a speculative theory; it is, as Maritain has said, a way of salvation. Its purpose is not merely to know about God, but to know God as God knows himself, to participate in the divine nature. But there is a flaw in this philosophy. Though Sankara has understood the true nature of God, he does not allow sufficiently for the reality of the creature; he lacks in fact the idea of creation. The world to him is Maya; it is an illusion. Our error is that we mistake the forms of this world for reality; when the illusion has been dispelled (and this is the work of Yoga), then we shall know ourselves and all things as they really are, that is as Brahma. In such a view the creature is lost in the Creator; there is "really" no creature at all.

But if, as Father Johanns has said in his great work, *To Christ Through the Vedanta,* we introduce into this philosophy the idea of creation, and assert that man is separated from God not merely by an "illusion" but by sin; and if we see in Christ the true Atma, who has delivered man from sin and united him to God in his Self, then the philosophy of the Vedanta gains its full significance and can be seen to form the basis for a perfectly Christian view of life.

Hardly less remarkable from a Christian point of view

than the Indian concept of the Atma is the Chinese idea of
the Tao. The word Tao simply means the "way", and
was used in early Chinese texts for the "way of heaven"
to signify the norm of right conduct. But in the *Tao te
Ching*, the "Book of the Way and its Power", as Arthur
Waley translates it, it came to be used absolutely for the
Principle which governs the universe. It is the beginning
and end of all things, at once transcendent and immanent,
sustaining and directing all things by its inherent power and
yet so utterly beyond them that it cannot even properly be
named. Perhaps it comes nearer than anything to the
Hebrew conception of Wisdom, which was with God in
the beginning and contains within itself the principles of all
things, while at the same time it pervades all things and
leads them to their end.

It is of great interest that in a recent Chinese translation
of the New Testament by the Catholic convert Dr Wu, the
first lines of St John's Gospel have been translated, "In
the beginning was the Tao, and the Tao was with God and
the Tao was God". In thus substituting the Chinese Tao
for the Greek Logos, which we translate the "Word", Dr
Wu has placed Chinese philosophy in the same relation to
the Gospel as Greek philosophy was placed originally by
St John's use of the word Logos. It cannot be doubted that
in using this word St John had in mind the Hebrew word
signifying the "word of God", which had come to the
Prophets of old and which St John declares has now been
manifested in the person of Christ. But in using the Greek
word Logos, signifying speech or reason, St John immediately brought the Hebrew revelation into relation with
Greek philosophy.

This was in fact the precise point at which the Hebrew
revelation made contact with Greek philosophy and set in
motion the whole development of Christian theology. Not
long after St John we find St Justin Martyr affirming that
the same Word or Logos which had been revealed in Christ
was known also to Socrates and Heraclitus as the Reason

which governs the universe. What the Law had been to the Jews, as Clement of Alexandria was to say, philosophy had been to the Greeks, a " Pedagogue " to lead them to Christ. This is surely a principle of incalculable importance when we try to place the great philosophical systems of China and India in relation to the Gospel.

We are aware more than ever now of the vast numbers of men who have never come within the sphere of the Hebrew or Christian revelation, and it becomes urgent to be able to understand their relation to it. In the light of this principle enunciated by St Justin, which was held also by Clement of Alexandria and others after him, we are able to affirm that from the very beginning God has been leading all men by means of his Word or Wisdom, which is the divine principle of Reason governing the universe. A knowledge of this divine Law is to be found inscribed in the heart of all men, as St Paul declared, and there are traces of it to be found in all the known religions of mankind.

In the Hindu conception of the Atma and the Chinese conception of the Tao we have perhaps the most profound of all insights into this mystery, by which mankind has been prepared for its final revelation in Christ. If these ideas could be interpreted in the full light of divine revelation it is possible that they would lead to a development in theology no less significant than its original development through the influence of Greek philosophy.

This is not merely a question of introducing some new concepts into western theology, but of introducing a new way of thought and a new outlook on life. For centuries now Christianity has developed in a westerly direction, taking on an ever more western character of thought and expression. If it is ever to penetrate deeply into the East it will have to find a correspondingly eastern form, in which the genius of the peoples of the East will be able to find expression. For Christianity will never realise its full stature as a genuine Catholicism, that is, as the universal religion of mankind, until it has incorporated into itself all that is

valid and true in all the different religious traditions. If
we believe that in Christ is to be found the revelation of
Truth itself, then we must recognise that all truth wherever
it is to be found is contained implicitly in Christianity. As
St Justin Martyr again said, "All truth wherever it is
found belongs to us as Christians."

This means that we must have a deep respect for the
truth which is to be found in all forms of religion and be
always ready to learn in order that we ourselves may be
able to understand the full significance of our own religion.
Nor must we think that our religion must necessarily be
restricted to any of its present forms of thought or expression. The Catholic Church, as Pope Benedict the Fifteenth
has said, is neither Latin nor Greek nor Slav, but universal.
There was once a Greek and a Slavonic Christianity as
orthodox and catholic as our Latin Christianity, and there
is no reason why there should not be a Chinese, an Indian
or an African Christianity. There are already Chinese and
Indian Cardinals; there is no reason why there should not
some day be a Chinese, an Indian or an African Pope.

In the same way with regard to the differences which
exist among Christians we have to learn to recognise that
every form of Christianity embodies some aspect of the
truth. Every heresy is the assertion of some aspect of
Christian truth which has been isolated from the rest and so
has developed into error. We have to learn not only to
reject the error but to recognise also the truth by which it
lives. George Fox and the Quakers understood the mystery
of the indwelling presence of the Holy Spirit and the inner
light of contemplation, while rejecting the sacraments.
Wesley and his followers understood the saving power of
Christ and the grace of conversion, while they came to
reject the hierarchy of the Church. The Church of England
while basing itself on the Bible as the unique source of
revelation like all Protestant churches, retained the elements
of liturgy and hierarchy, but rejected the authority of the
Pope. Each has something to bring to the Church, its

characteristic piety, its devotion to the Bible, to preaching, to the liturgy, to the person of Christ. For the Church, though she possesses all truth essentially, yet still awaits her accidental perfection. She has to be extended to all people in order that she may manifest all the riches of Christ. For Catholicism cannot be true to its name, if it is anything less than a universal religion, in which all truth is embodied and every form of piety and holiness is manifested in the unity of the one Body of Christ.

The divisions which at present exist among Christians are but one aspect of that deeper conflict which divides mankind and dismembers the Body of Christ. For we must always remember that the bounds of the Church are co-extensive with mankind. When the Word of God, who is that Wisdom by which and through which and for which all things exist, assumed a human nature, he came to unite all mankind in one Body in himself. There is no man from the beginning to the end of the world, who does not receive grace from Christ and who is not called to eternal life in him. He is the true light which enlightens every man coming into the world. It is the same Spirit which from the beginning of history has been leading all men by his grace; it is the same Word, which enlightens them through their reason and conscience and prepares them for the revelation of himself. All men, therefore, who are guided by their reason and conscience and follow the light which has been given them, are truly by their implicit faith and desire disciples of Christ and vitally related to his Church. And yet while we hold to the absolute universality of grace and believe that no one is deprived of it save by his own deliberate choice, we must hold with equal certainty that God chose to reveal himself to one particular people and established among them the unique way of salvation. All religious traditions contain some elements of the truth, but there is only one absolutely true religion; all religions have taught something of the way of salvation, but there is only one absolute Way. Christ is the Way, the Truth and the Life, and without him no man comes to the Father.

In the same way we must believe that there is one Church, which was founded by Christ upon the Rock of Peter, to be the way of salvation for all mankind. In this Church all those elements of truth which have been dispersed among the different peoples of the earth are gathered into unity; it is the centre from which they derive their value and significance. The Church with her hierarchy and sacraments is the sole basis of unity for mankind, for it is this visible, hierarchical Church which constitutes the mystical Body of Christ on earth. Her ministers and her sacraments are simply the chosen instruments of divine grace, the means by which men are incorporated into the Body of Christ and made to participate in the light of his truth. It is the building up of this Body of Christ, this City of God, which is the real purpose of human life. Material civilisations and social cultures have their rise and fall, but their value lies simply in their capacity to assist mankind in its progress towards this City of God. This is the standard by which they are to be judged. Our own civilisation will pass, as those of the past have done; there is no need either to fear or to regret it. For the "schema", the "outward form" of this world, as St Paul called it, is passing away; but beneath the outward form there is being built up continuously the Body of Christ, which is the unity of mankind in Truth and Charity. It is a hidden and mysterious process, which will only be realised in its fullness when this world of space and time has passed away altogether. Then we shall see the Church as it really is, as the fulfilment of the whole creation, the achievement of man's destiny by his participation in the life of God.

But what, it may be said, of all the scandals of Church history, the evil within the Church, the corruption of Popes and bishops, of clergy and people, the atrocities of the Crusades, of the Inquisition and the wars of religion?

There can be but one answer to this question. This was the mystery of the Crucifixion of the Body of Christ. Christ was crucified once in his natural body, but he is crucified daily in his mystical body, the Church. This is what all Christians experience daily in their lives. Christ is crucified in us when that Truth and Charity, which constitute the essence of the Church, are betrayed by us. The Church remains essentially holy, but we who make up the members of the Church betray her by our sins.

Not long ago Mr Middleton Murry wrote a book in which he spoke of "the betrayal of Christ by the Churches". To this Father Gerald Vann wrote a reply in which he spoke of "the betrayal of the Church by the Christians". Both were concerned with the same facts, but Mr Murry spoke as a Protestant, Father Vann as a Catholic. It is impossible for Christ to be betrayed by the Church, because the Church is His Body and lives by His life, which is essentially holy. But the members of that Body may sin and so betray both Christ and the Church, and this is the situation in which we find ourselves. We are all more or less guilty, and the responsibility for the world's misery lies with the Christian people as much as with anybody.

All the great errors of our civilisation from the Reformation to the Russian revolution have arisen because of the failure of Christians to embody the truth of Christ in their lives. If Communism presents itself now as the great enemy of our civilisation, it is because it embodies, in however distorted a manner, that thirst for social justice which Christianity failed to satisfy. When Marx declared that the aim of Communism was to "realise the essence of man" in the classless society, he was proclaiming what is the real aim of Christianity itself. For Christ is truly the Perfect Man, in whom all the potentialities of human nature are realised, and it is by membership of his Body, that we become part of a social organism in which all the conflicts of class and race and religion are transcended, and man realises his true nature as a son of God.

Such is the vision of the Church which Catholicism presents to us. It corresponds with all the deepest needs of mankind at the present day. While remaining true to that tradition of faith and doctrine which has been handed down from the beginning, it seeks to embrace all that is true in modern science and ancient philosophy. It envisages mankind in the whole length and breadth of its history as part of a divine plan, through which the destiny of man is to be fulfilled in a new order of being transcending this world of space and time. It faces the full tragedy of the situation in which we find ourselves, and finds the source of conflict in human life in the free choice of the will by which man becomes subject to sin.

To be a Christian is to accept the responsibility for sin not only in oneself but in others also. It is to recognise that we all bear the responsibility for one another.

To be a monk is to take up deliberately the burden of this responsibility, and to seek to share in the sufferings of Christ for the sake of His Body, which is the Church. It is to be alive to all the needs of mankind, but to try to respond to them not by an external activity, but by entering by prayer into the heart of that mystery of sacrifice by which the redemption of the world is achieved. Thus may we come to fulfil the words with which St Benedict concludes the Prologue to his Rule : " That never departing from His teaching and persevering in the monastery until death, we may so share by patience in the sufferings of Christ, that we may deserve to be partakers of his kingdom."

HEAVEN'S GATE

In the palaeolithic caves which have been discovered in the south of France it has been found that there are long winding passages leading from the front of the cave by a difficult and often dangerous path into the inmost recesses of the rock, and there in the darkness of the interior are to be found those drawings of animals which astonish us with their power and beauty. Why was it that these pictures were drawn in the darkness of the interior where they could only be seen by the light of a torch of moss dipped in animal fat? Miss Rachel Levy in her *Gate of Horn* has given us the answer. The pictures on the wall were the sacred images by means of which it was believed that man could enter into communion with the divine powers, and the long, winding difficult passage to the interior represented the dark and difficult approach to the divine Mystery.

We find this symbolism continued all through neolithic times, in the megalithic temples and in the ritual dances of primitive peoples today; always there is the laborious approach to the sacred place where the encounter with the divine mystery is to take place. But it is in the Egyptian Pyramids that the full significance of this symbolism is revealed. In the interior of the Pyramid there is a long winding stairway with many twists and turns by which it was intended that the Pharaoh should make his ascent to the summit, and on the walls were depicted the scenes of the Pharaoh's journey through the underworld. Here it becomes clear that the winding passage is the path of man's ascent to God, and this path is a journey through the realms of death leading to the place where man ascends above this world and enters into immortality.

Thus from the earliest times, of which we have any knowledge, it seems to have been understood that our life in this world is a journey towards God. The journey is from the mouth of the cave, which represents the external world, into the interior which appears as darkness; it is the passage from the outer to the inner world. It is this journey which is represented by the descent of Aeneas into the underworld in search of his Father. The same motive appears in the Odyssey as the return of the Hero by a long and difficult voyage home, where his wife awaits him. Or again it is found in the legend of Theseus making his way to the centre of the Labyrinth in search of his Bride.

All these stories are symbols of the same mystery of the search for God which is at the same time the return to our true home. It is represented sometimes as a new birth, a return to the womb, or again as a descent into the tomb by which we rise again to a new life. Always it has been understood that our life in this world, as Keats said, is a " perpetual allegory "; everything has meaning only in reference to something beyond. We are, as Plato saw it, like men in a cave who see reality reflected on the walls of the cave, as in a cinema. The illusion of this world is that by which we mistake the figures on the screen for reality. This is the sin of idolatry, for idolatry is nothing but the worship of images, the mistaking the image of truth for Truth itself.

Scientific materialism in the modern world is the precise counterpart of pagan idolatry in the ancient world; it is the substitution of appearance for reality. For science as such is only concerned with phenomena, that is, with things as they appear to the senses : its function is, in the Greek phrase, to " save the phenomena ", to account for the appearance of things. But of the reality which underlies the appearance, of the real nature of things, science can give us no knowledge at all. We only begin to awake to reality when we realise that the material world, the world of space and time, as it appears to our senses, is nothing but a sign and a symbol of a mystery which infinitely transcends it. That

is why the images in the palaeolithic cave were painted in
the dark; it is only when we have passed beyond the world
of images that we can enter into communion with the
mystery which lies beyond.

This sense of a mystery transcending the world, of which
this world, as we know it, is only a sign, is the root of all
religion. It underlies the religion of primitive man; it is
embodied in the ancient myths and legends; it is found at
the basis both of Egyptian and Babylonian religion, and it
takes shape finally in the mystery religions which are found
all over the ancient world. In these religions the cycle of
life and death in nature, the passage of the seasons through
the death of winter to rebirth in the spring, is seen as a
symbol of man's passage through death into life, of his
rebirth to immortality.

In the great awakening which took place in so many
different parts of the world in the first millennium before
Christ, which Karl Jaspers called the "axial period" of
human history, the full significance of this religion comes
to light. It was then that as by a kind of universal awakening the real meaning of life seems to have dawned upon the
human mind. In India and China, in Persia and in Greece,
a movement of thought began, by which mankind finally
pierced through the barrier of the senses and discovered the
mystery of the world which lies beyond. This was the great
discovery which brought enlightenment to the Buddha;
this was the source of the inspiration of the Upanishads and
the tradition of the Vedanta : this was what was revealed in
China as the Tao and in Greece as the Logos.

To each people the mystery was revealed in a different
way. To the Indian it came rather as sense of the utter
unreality of the phenomenal world in comparison with
the reality of that which lay beyond. To the Chinese it
appeared as a principle of harmony, a cosmic order uniting man and nature in an organic society. The Greek saw
it as a law of Reason by which "all things are steered

through all things ", which gave rise to Plato's conception
of the " world of ideas " and to Plotinus's vision of the One,
transcending all thought and all being.

Thus from the beginning of the world, as far as we can
judge, man has known himself to be in the presence of a
mystery. He has expressed his sense of the mystery in myth
and legend; he has striven to approach the mystery by
prayer and sacrifice; he has tried to apprehend it by
thought. But at a certain point in history the Mystery
chose to reveal itself. It manifested itself by signs and
wonders to a particular people; it declared its will through
the voice of the Prophets. It was revealed as a Person
whose will is justice and whose nature is love. It appeared
on earth in a human nature and revealed in that human
nature the destiny to which man had through all the centuries aspired. For Christ came to recapitulate all the stages
of human history, to sum up in himself the destiny of mankind. It was no accident that he was born in a cave. He
travelled the whole of that long, difficult and laborious
path by which we have to return to the Father. He went
down like Aeneas into the underworld; he passed through
death into life; he ascended above this world of space and
time into the divine presence.

But Christ did not open this path for himself alone. On
the day before he was to die, he instituted a rite by which
his disciples might be enabled to follow him on the same
path by which he had travelled. He took bread and wine,
the symbols of sacrifice throughout the ancient world, and
made them the sacramental means by which his disciples
might share in the mystery of his death and enter into a
new life with him.

It is here in the sacrifice, accomplished once in time on
the Cross and renewed sacramentally day by day under
the symbols of bread and wine, that all religion finds its
fulfilment. He fulfilled all those ancient sacrifices by which
man had striven to approach the mystery; he fulfilled all

the ancient legends of the return of man to God. For what was it that took place in the interior darkness of the cave? There can be no doubt of the answer; it is the mystery of sacrifice. At the centre of all religion in the holy place, where the encounter with the divine mystery is to take place, stands the altar of sacrifice.

And what is sacrifice? To sacrifice is literally to " make a thing sacred "; it is to take something out of common use and to make it over to God. It is a symbolic act by which we recognise that everything in this world derives from another order of being and seek to enter into communion with that other world. But the outward thing which is sacrificed can never be more than a sign of inward offering; what we desire has to take place in the centre of our own being, in the darkness of the interior where alone we can encounter the God who is hidden in the depths of the soul. We have to pass beyond all the images of the senses, beyond all the concepts of the mind, beyond ourselves, if we are really to find God.

But this is precisely what of ourselves we can never do. We have become separated from the centre of our being, we have lost the thread in the maze. We wander endlessly exploring the mouth of the cave, living in a world of shadows. Never has mankind experienced more appallingly than at the present day this sense of separation from reality; the world has become a nightmare from which there seems to be no escape.

Where then is the clue to the centre? Where is the Golden String to be found? The Golden String is Christ; he is the clue to the centre. The sacrifice of Christ is the central event of human history; it is the event which alone gives meaning to life. It was in the Resurrection of Christ that the illusion of this world was shattered and mankind was set free from the bondage of space and time. If we have lost the way and become enslaved again by the appearance of this world, it is because we have deliberately

turned our backs on the truth. We have denied the validity
of sacrifice and therefore we have become haunted with a
sense of guilt.

The human imagination has always been haunted by the
feeling that we must die in order that we may live; that we
have to be born again. To be a Christian is to accept this
mystery of death and resurrection in one's own life; it is to
pass through the world of appearances into the realm of
Being. It is to commit oneself to the view that the world as
we know it is not the world for which we are created. It is
to confess that we are "strangers and exiles on earth"; that
we have here "no abiding city". Already science has
begun to recognise that the outward forms of matter, the
molecules and atoms, the protons and electrons with which
it deals, are only a kind of algebra, a symbolic representation of certain elemental powers whose real nature we do
not know. We know that we ourselves, and the whole
universe of which we are a part, are in a state of evolution,
passing continually from one state of being to another.
Everything is subject to the same law of transformation.

But what is the end of this process? Of this science can
tell us nothing, but divine revelation comes to our aid. It
tells us that the whole of this world of space and time is
destined to pass away; there is to be "a new heaven and a
new earth", where "time will be no more". Mankind is to
be reunited in a new order of Being, a society transcending
the limitations of this world, in which man will participate
in the life of God. We are to enter into the vision of God,
that vision of all things in their eternal truth, which is the
object of all our quest on earth.

And yet when we have said this, we have to confess that
the mystery remains. Nothing which we can conceive of
God or of eternal life can have more than a remote resemblance to the reality. Christianity does not explain the
mystery; it only opens up the way of approach to the mystery. God himself remains the unfathomable mystery, the

incomprehensible Being. Nothing which we say of him can ever be more than a remote analogy of the truth. The very name of "God" is only a convenience of speech. Even if we say that God "exists", we have to admit that his existence is of a different kind from anything that we know. If we say that he is wisdom, truth, goodness, beauty, love, we have to acknowledge that though he is all that we can conceive of all these things, yet he is infinitely beyond our conception. Even the dogmas of the Church, of the Trinity, the Incarnation, the Eucharist, do not define the mystery properly speaking. They only express in human terms what he has chosen to reveal concerning himself. They are, like the sacraments themselves, signs of a mystery which cannot be expressed. And yet we need these signs if we are to approach the mystery. They are in the language of Blake's poem, "Jerusalem's Wall"; they are the ramparts which defend the City of God. It has been the tragedy of the modern world that we have thought that by breaking down the walls we could open the City to all men. But we have only succeeded in profaning the truth and emptying life of its meaning. For the divine mystery can only be approached by faith, and the dogmas and sacraments of the Church are the walls in which the gate of faith, which is "heaven's gate", is to be found. The moment we attempt to enter of ourselves, to do without the Church, we shut ourselves out of the City. But when we learn to accept the dogmas and sacraments of the Church, then we can enter by faith into the heart of the mystery; we can pass through the sign to the thing signified, through the image to the reality.

Thus the Church herself is the great sacramental mystery. Her hierarchy, her sacraments, her dogmas, are nothing but signs and instruments by which the divine mystery is manifested to mankind. If we stop short at the sign, then it becomes a wall which separates us from the truth; but if we enter by the gate of faith through the wall, then we discover the City of God. We shall never rebuild our civilisation until we begin to build up again the walls which have been pulled down, and accept the Church as the guardian of the divine mystery. Then science and philosophy and art will once again recover their significance by being related to the true end of human life. Without the recognition of an end which totally transcends this world, science can only become a system of idolatry, philosophy can only contemplate the meaninglessness of human existence, and art can only disintegrate into fragments. But once we place the Church at the centre of existence as the guardian of divine truth and divine love, then the whole world recovers its meaning.

Then we realise that the whole universe is a sacrament, which mirrors the divine reality; that each created thing, though nothing in itself, is of infinite value and significance because it is the sign of a mystery, which is enshrined in the depths of its being. Then every human being is known to be not merely an isolated individual carried along on the flux of time and doomed to extinction, but a member of a divine society, working out its destiny in space and time and subject to all the tragic consequences of subservience to the material world, but destined to transcend the limitations of time and space and mortality and to enter into that fullness of life where there shall be " neither mourning nor weeping nor pain any more ". The suffering of this world can have no meaning as long as we attempt to judge it in the light of this present time. We are like people who hear snatches of music, which they have no means of relating to the symphony as a whole. But when we have passed beyond the conditions of this present life we shall then have that integral knowledge in which the whole is known in every part and every part is seen to mirror the whole.

This is a certainty which only faith can give, but even now we can begin to discern something of the truth. For love can give us a kind of knowledge which is beyond both faith and reason. The divine mystery is ultimately a mystery of love, and it reveals itself to love alone. It is only if we are prepared to give ourselves totally in love that Love will give itself totally to us. Then we shall discover that the power which "moves the sun and the other stars" is indeed a power of love; that it is this that lies at the heart of our human existence and shapes our lives. But it is a love which revealed itself in an agony of self-surrender on the Cross, and only makes itself known to those who are prepared to make the same surrender. For the love of God is not a mild benevolence; it is a consuming fire. To those who resist it it becomes an eternal torment; to those who are willing to face its demands, it becomes a fire that cleanses and purifies; those whom it has once penetrated, it transforms into itself.

Perhaps no modern writer has fathomed the depths of suffering in the human soul with such insight as Dostoevsky in *The Brothers Karamazov*. In those three brothers the modern soul is laid bare in all its passion of revolt, its cynicism and intellectual doubt, its generosity and idealism. Dostoevsky had experienced the depths of suffering in his own life and had learned the mystery of redemption through love. It is surely significant that he looked for the redemption of the world to the Russian peasant and the Russian monk. No country has gone further than Russia since the time of Dostoevsky in the rejection of God, of Christ and the Church, in the rejection of that wisdom which belonged to the peasant and the monk. But we have all tried to build our civilisation without these foundations, without contact either with the earth or with heaven. If we are ever to find peace either in ourselves or in the world we shall have to learn again that ancient wisdom which alone can give man peace with nature and with God, and which was summed up by Dostoevsky in the words of the Prior of the monastery in which the Brothers Karamazov met: "Brothers, have no fear of men's sin. Love a man even in his sin, for that is the semblance of divine love, and is the highest love on earth. Love all God's creation, the whole and every grain of sand in it. Love every leaf and every ray of God's light. Love the animals, love the plants, love everything. If you love everything you will perceive the divine mystery in things. Once you perceive it, you will begin to comprehend it better every day. And you will come at last to love the whole world with an all-embracing love."

PUBLISHER'S NOTE

Believing that readers of *The Golden String* might like to know what has happened to its author, we have added some details of the events of his life during the years which have passed since his ordination.

Until 1947, Bede Griffiths remained at Prinknash, then he left to become Prior of St Michael's Abbey, Farnborough; from where he went as Novice Master in 1951 to another new foundation, Pluscarden Priory, Elgin.

In 1955, an Indian Benedictine monk asked him to go to India and help in founding a Benedictine monastery there. How much this prospect must have attracted him we can guess from what he has written . . . "Certainly from the Christian point of view the importance of Indian philosophy can hardly be over-estimated." (p. 171). The Abbot of Prinknash gave him permission to accept the invitation and for two years he lived in a small monastery outside Bangalore, where he had many contacts with Hindus. It proved, however, impossible to make the intended foundation there, so Bede Griffiths joined up with a Belgian Cistercian monk, Francis Mahieu, who had also gone to India with the idea of establishing a religious foundation. He, curiously enough, had been Novice Master at Caldey Abbey, the monastery taken over by the Belgian Cistercians of Scourmont Abbey when the Prinknash Community had left to settle in Gloucestershire.

In March 1958, the two monks settled at Kurisumala Ashram (*Ashram* is the Indian word for a monastery) in the high range of Kerala, South India. Soon two novices joined them and six years later their number had grown to fifteen. At the start they lived in a palm leaf hut; later they erected a stone-built house and became self-supporting, thanks to a dairy farm.

The Community belongs to the Syrian rite, that is to say that canonically they are an Eastern monastery under a Syrian Bishop. This is because most of the Catholic Indians of Kerala—they claim to have been evangelised by St Thomas the Apostle—belong to this rite. The monks have their liturgy in Syrian, but, as they have the right to use the vernacular, they also make use of English and of the local language, Malayalam.

Basically, they follow the Rule of St Benedict, with a Cistercian observance, but, since the Eastern Monasteries are not bound to any one particular rule (indeed each monastery has its *typikon,* which it is allowed to frame for itself) and the purpose of the Kerala community is to offer a Christian life of prayer as closely identified as possible with local customs, the monks use various Eastern rules, try to adapt themselves to the tradition of the Eastern Christian tradition, and also where possible to follow customs common to the innumerable Hindu Ashrams which exist throughout the country.

For instance, they wear the ochre or saffron-coloured *kavi* (habit) of the Sannyasis (the word means renunciation and those to whom it is applied are the Hindu equivalent of monks); they go barefoot, sit on the floor, own practically no furniture, keep to a strict vegetarian diet and eat with their hands.

To give a picture of their daily life one might recall the description given by Mahatma Ghandi of a Cistercian monastery in South Africa, which he visited at an early stage in his life: " They get up at 2.30 a.m.; they eat a purely vegetarian diet : they strictly observe the silence; only two or three go to the nearest market or speak to visitors . . . they add a calling to their learning. They are gardeners, carpenters, tailors, shoe makers, cooks, etc. I still live much under the spell of the sweet silence of their calls. It would be my very ideal to found such an institute, but it needs followers who would dedicate body and soul for all their lives."

After several years at Kurisumala Ashram, Bede Griffiths and two other monks moved from Kerala to another Ashram in Tamil Nadu, the old Madras State, which had been founded by two French Fathers, pioneers in the attempt to adapt the monastic life in India to the traditional forms of Indian life and prayer. Here their community life centres on the personal prayer of each member, although they meet together three times a day for informal prayer in which there are also readings from the Scriptures of different religions. There is thus a daily reminder of the relationship between the different religions and their search for Truth.